To John Nesbo,
Tracy & I wish you Merry
Christmas 2004.
Norma B. Ashby

Movie Stars & Rattlesnakes

The Heyday of Montana LIVE Television

by Norma Beatty Ashby

Happy Birthday Dad! 2005
Shawn, Tracy, Alex & Hunter

FARCOUNTRY
PRESS

*To my beloved family and friends, near and far.
And to my favorite state, Montana.*

COVER: Norma in 1968 in front of the set featuring a photograph of Saint Mary's Lake in Glacier National Park. Small photos, from left: Norma with Joan Crawford, Bob Hope, Johnny Cash and Roy Rogers.

ISBN: 1-56037-365-2 (hardcover)
ISBN: 1-56037-366-0 (softcover)
© 2004 Farcountry Press
Photographs, except as noted, are from the Norma Ashby collection.

For Montana Centennial Dinner statement from John Steinbeck, this is the approved copyright: Copyright (c) 1964 by John Steinbeck. Reprinted with permission by McIntosh and Otis, Inc.; *Travels With Charley* by John Steinbeck, copyright (c) 1961, 1962 by The Curtis Publishing Co., (c) 1962 by John Steinbeck, renewed (c) 1990 by Elaine Steinbeck, Thom Steinbeck and John Steinbeck 1V. Used by permission of Viking Penguin, a division of Penguin Group (USA) Inc.

Symbols of Montana © 1989 by Rex C. Myers and Norma B. Ashby. Montana Historical Society Foundation, Helena, Montana.

This book may not be reproduced in whole or in part by any means (with the exception of short quotes for the purpose of review) without the permission of the publisher.

For more information about our books write Farcountry Press,
P.O. Box 5630, Helena, MT 59604; call (800) 821-3874;
or visit www.farcountrypress.com.

Created, produced, and designed in the United States.
Printed in Canada.

09 08 07 06 05 04

1   2   3   4   5

Contents

Acknowledgments 4

Foreword 6

Chapter One—Norma Ashby LIVE! 9

Chapter Two—On Camera: Celebrities 43

Chapter Three—On Camera: Montanans 77

Chapter Four—On Location 103

Chapter Five—Off Camera 119

Chapter Six—Moving On 149

Index 158

Acknowledgments

This book could not have been written without the assistance, support and encouragement of many people.

First for helping to develop within me a love of writing, I would like to credit my late mother, Ella Mehmke, who enjoyed writing letters and who inspired me to write my first book at the age of twelve, a mystery, which is still unpublished. My sister, Annemarie, who was editor of our high school newspaper, also inspired me as did Faye Kirkpatrick, my high school journalism teacher; J. D. Holmes, my next door neighbor who worked for The Associated Press, when I was growing up in Helena; John Willard, a newspaper reporter, whom I met at a high school career night when I chose journalism as my future career; Al Gaskill, editor of the Helena *Independent Record*, who was my boss for three summers when I was a cub reporter.

For encouraging me in writing this book, I have many thanks to give to my husband Shirley, my Aunt Marge Elerding and Dave Walter, who read my manuscript and gave me helpful suggestions; Cindy Kittredge, who taught me how to be disciplined in writing a book; and Terry Dwyer who inspired me with his experiences in writing his books.

Special friends who have been my cheerleaders are: Sherry Beaver, Bonnie Donohue, Marianne Granlie, Glenda McLaughlin, Jane Meyer, Mary Jo Olson, Gwen Swedberg, and Margaret Towne.

I also owe a great deal to Dan Snyder for writing the foreword and all my other friends in broadcasting and the rest of the media.

Invaluable assistance was given to me by April Hansen and Roger Call, who helped me with the elec-

Norma Beatty Ashby, 1989.

tronic challenges I had with writing and compiling the manuscript entirely on my computer; Sara Kegel and John Sinn, in the reference department of the Great Falls Public Library; and J. Michael Keyes, with Preston/Gates/Ellis.

To Farcountry Press for seeing the potential in my manuscript and becoming my publisher: Brad Hurd, Lisa Mee, Linda Netschert and Kathy Springmeyer. Kudos especially to my editor Caroline Patterson, who always saw the humor in each step of the process and gave my book its title.

Here are others to whom I am indebted to for giving me permission to include material within the pages of this book:

> Bobby Burgess; the *Cascade Courier*; *Great Falls Tribune*; Toni Knudson; Chet Huntley Collection, K. Ross Toole Archives, The University of Montana-Missoula; KRTV Communications; Inc., Robert Lind; The Margaret Chase Smith Library; McIntosh & Otis, Inc.; J.K. Ralston Studio Foundation, and the numerous individuals who supplied dates and details for the myriad questions I needed answered.

Finally to all my guests who told me their stories and to all my viewers who watched me all those years on television, thank you. Without you, there wouldn't have been this story to tell. If this book triggers a happy memory or two, than my efforts will have been worth it.

Foreword

You are about to meet a remarkable woman. And, through her eyes, you will meet a potpourri of interesting people. When I hired Norma, I had no idea what to expect. She came highly recommended, but she had no television experience and I was launching a new one-hour live talk show with her as my co-host. On that first day, we were seated on the set, side by side, under the bright lights that were necessary in those days. The theme music signaled thirty seconds to go, before the studio camera's red light would go on, cuing us to begin day one of *Today in Montana*.

I turned to look at Norma. She turned to look at me. In her eyes, I didn't see fear, I saw stark terror. She asked me if I had any last-minute advice. I did. With ten seconds to go, I gave her two suggestions. She burst out laughing, her eyes sparkled and she began like an old pro.

Norma was destined for the show. She had a natural talent for performing, coupled with a pleasant personality. She warmed to people and people warmed to her. It's the variety of people, what they say and how they say it, that makes a show. Over the years, Norma developed a knack for creating an interesting and sometimes exciting show.

Part of the fun in this book are the quotes from the celebrities she interviewed. Bob Hope's quips about Ronald Reagan. Patricia Neal's love for Montana actor Gary Cooper. Vincent Price's advice on how to stay young. The best, however, was her interview with Robert Goulet. To this day, she can't talk about Robert Goulet without gurgling. Next time you see Norma, tell her you want to hear the Robert Goulet gurgle.

I was always amazed at Norma's memory because in the early days before videotape, she had to write these memories down after the show. This book would never have happened if it hadn't been for Norma's persistence in compiling notes. With these notes and the thousands of pictures she took, she inadvertently became KRTV's historian.

Norma could be very persuasive when she wanted something or someone on the show. I told her one day, "Norma, you're wasting your time in the programming, you could make a lot more money in sales." I'm glad she didn't take my advice, but after she retired....well, she'll tell you in her own words.

The persuasiveness paid off when she got Chet Huntley to narrate a script she wrote on Helena entitled *Last Chance Gulch*. Since she was born in Helena, this was special to her. You'll enjoy knowing how she met Chet Huntley. Chet, who was also a native Montanan, never forgot his roots and wrote a wonderful piece that Norma has included.

She'll also tell you about John Steinbeck's love affair with Montana.

Norma's love for Montana is all through this book. As you will see, she carried it on for twenty-six years. It's a tribute to her that the three owners after me each bought into her vision and kept the show going.

On a personal note, when I sold the stations and left after ten years, I thought KRTV would be history in my life. But, the ever-organizing Norma decided that we ought to have a reunion every year. And we do to this day.

What she hasn't told you in this book is that I finagled a way to get her on the air with me again. When Shodair Hospital, our children's hospital in Helena asked me to host a twenty-one-hour telethon, I agreed to accept if my co-host was Norma. She agreed and we did the telethon for six years. It worked, and worked well, because of the chemistry between us.

In 1984, Norma was the object of a charity roast in Great Falls. I delivered this toast instead.

What is a Norma?
You might say she's a special kind,
Not a will-of-the-wisp, but one with a most determined mind.
Proud of her Montana heritage elite,
The friendliest kind you'll ever meet.
Festooned for the Centennial or as an Indian princess,
With exhaustive research, she'll give us historical glimpses.
To the end of the earth she'll go,
 For that something different on her TV show.
From a rattlesnake cut open with all of its gore,
To reindeer prancing through, leaving droppings on the floor.
Her Christmas shows were the highlight of the year,
And for Norma that meant family, kids and a tear.
But whether it was Christmas or not,
Sentimental Norma just always cried a lot.
We salute you, Norma Beatty Ashby, hostess,
Emcee extraordinair, great and grandiousus.
Will *Today in Montana* last? Don't be silly,
Three bosses she's had from Snyder to Sample to Lilly.
With awards and honors and grateful thanks, from you
Friends and fans and peers,
A toast to you Norma for another twenty-two years.

—Dan Snyder, August 2004

Norma in broadcast booth in the School of Journalism
at the University of Montana-Missoula in 1954.

— 1 —
Norma Beatty **LIVE!**

I was "discovered" at Graham & Ross, a farm supply store in Great Falls, Montana, by Ed Kolman, an ad salesman for KRTV. I had returned to Great Falls in November 1961 when my sister Annemarie Roth became terminally ill with cancer. I was working at the farm supply store because it was the only job I could find. Even though I had worked for four years at *LIFE* Magazine and *MD Medical Newsmagazine* in New York and had a journalism degree from the University of Montana in Missoula, there were no openings at the Great Falls Tribune, KARR Radio or at Public Relations Associates where I had applied.

That day at the farm supply store, Ed mentioned that Dan Snyder, the owner of the four-year-old television station, KRTV, was thinking of starting a daily TV show and he was looking for a hostess. Kolman encouraged me to apply.

My job interview on February 14, 1962, was with Paul Crain, an amiable yet intense man who was general manager of KRTV. We were sitting in front of picture windows that overlooked the city of Great Falls.

He turned to me and asked, "What broadcasting experience have you had?"

I cleared my throat and said, "None."

He looked at me. "Why do you think you could do this job?"

I sat up straight and looked him in the eye. "I have always liked people and I have been asking questions since I could talk," I said. "Instead of saying, 'Mama' and 'Daddy,' I said, 'What's that?' and 'Who's that?'"

I was hired.

Dan Snyder, a tall, slim, handsome man with boundless energy and enthusiasm, observed our interview. He was a man who would

> *"There are just two things to remember and if you remember these two things you will go far in broadcasting. The first one is don't swear and the second one is don't pick your nose on the air."*

Dan Snyder and Norma Beatty on the first set for *Today in Montana,* featuring the Anaconda smokestack and the Great Falls' nightscape.
DEMIER STUDIO

have a lasting influence on my career. Five days later, on February 19, 1962, I was on the air from 8 to 9 a.m. with Dan Snyder on a daily one hour TV show called *Today in Montana*. That was the beginning of my career in broadcasting at KRTV in Great Falls, Montana, which spanned two and one-half decades from 1962-1988.

This was a unique era and a very exciting time to be part of this new medium. Television was in its infancy. Television was black and white. There were just two channels to choose from in Great Falls. There was no cable, no satellite dishes, no videotape, no scripts, and no teleprompters. Digital television had not even been dreamed of. Nearly everything was live except the film segments.

The first television station in Montana, KXLF in Butte, that was owned by Ed Craney, went on the air in 1953. KFBB, our competition, went on the air a year later. KRTV had been up and running since 1958.

I was paid $15 a show, $75 a week or $300 a month. In 1962, that was an adequate income for me. My rent for a furnished apartment was only $100 a month. My new Volkswagen cost me $1,800, which I had paid for with my savings from New York. Dan would often say to me that I could make more money in sales and although I did some selling, I always preferred my on-air work.

Our studio was a large tin-roofed Quonset hut, which worked well because of all the room. The one drawback was the noise. When it rained or hailed, the noise on the roof was difficult to mute during live broadcasts.

On our first *Today in Montana* set, we had a Great Falls night scene featuring the Anaconda smokestack as our backdrop. Dan and I sat at a desk with a microphone between us. We had a couch for our guests to sit on and a carpeted raised platform for our exercise girl to perform on. Edna Lockwood was our camerawoman, which was a tough job because the black and white camera was heavy to push around, even on rollers. Jeannie Hayden ran the boom mike, which we used for the exercise segment so the exercise "girl" (as they were called then) could move about freely. Barbara Taylor was our first exercise girl. Paul Crain delivered the news; Dan and I were co-hosts.

Paul Crain, KRTV general manager, doing the news on the first *Today in Montana* show on February 19, 1962.
DEMIER STUDIO

In the days before the show, we developed the set, contacted guests and Dan showed me how to put together a daily minute-by-minute format, which I typed on my upright Royal typewriter. Since I was new in town, Dan also helped me locate and contact guests.

With no on-air experience, I was very nervous that first day of the show. I had no script, just that one-page format in front of me. I asked Dan to give me some tips on what I should or shouldn't do on the air. Dan recalled later that when he looked at me, he didn't see just fear, but "stark terror" in my eyes. In order to help me relax, he said, "There are just two things to remember and if you remember these two things you will go far in broadcasting. The first one is don't swear and the second one is don't pick your nose on the air."

I burst out laughing.

Armed with this valuable advice, I launched my broadcasting

11

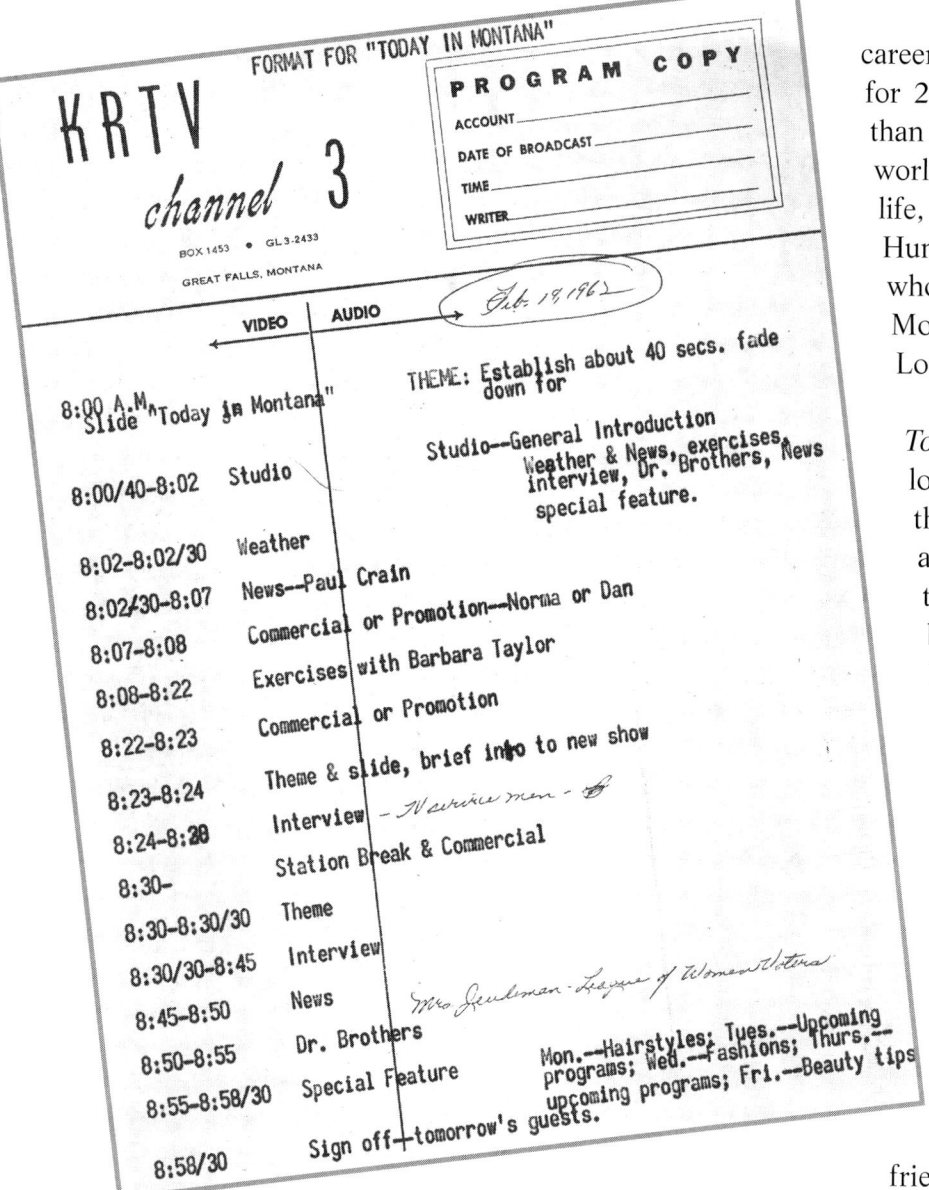

```
FORMAT FOR "TODAY IN MONTANA"

KRTV channel 3
BOX 1453 • GL 3-2433
GREAT FALLS, MONTANA

PROGRAM COPY
ACCOUNT
DATE OF BROADCAST
TIME
WRITER

                                    Feb. 19, 1962

VIDEO          AUDIO

8:00 A.M.      THEME: Establish about 40 secs. fade
Slide "Today in Montana"     down for

8:00/40-8:02   Studio    Studio—General Introduction
                          Weather & News, exercises,
                          interview, Dr. Brothers, News
                          special feature.

8:02-8:02/30   Weather
8:02/30-8:07   News—Paul Crain
8:07-8:08      Commercial or Promotion—Norma or Dan
8:08-8:22      Exercises with Barbara Taylor
8:22-8:23      Commercial or Promotion
8:23-8:24      Theme & slide, brief intro to new show
8:24-8:28      Interview — Servicemen —
8:30-          Station Break & Commercial
8:30-8:30/30   Theme
8:30/30-8:45   Interview     Mrs Juedeman - League of Women Voters
8:45-8:50      News
8:50-8:55      Dr. Brothers
8:55-8:58/30   Special Feature    Mon.—Hairstyles; Tues.—Upcoming
                                  programs; Wed.—Fashions; Thurs.—
                                  upcoming programs; Fri.—Beauty tips
8:58/30        Sign off—tomorrow's guests.
```

A copy of the actual typed-out format for the first *Today in Montana* program.

career, producing 260 shows a year for 26 years and interviewing more than 26,000 people from all over the world and from nearly every walk of life, ranging from newscaster Chet Huntley to prisoner Jerome Hayes, who was in solitary confinement at Montana State Prison in Deer Lodge.

Dan Snyder named our show *Today in Montana* because it followed the *Today Show* on NBC, the network with which we were affiliated. Dan also selected our theme song, "I Ain't Down Yet" by Meredith Willson, from the Broadway show, *The Unsinkable Molly Brown*. He had seen the show and thought it was a catchy tune. He liked it and so did I.

On February 19, 1962 at 8 a.m., the camera light went on for that first *Today in Montana* show. There was no time to be nervous. The studio clock could be my friend or my enemy and I decided to make it my friend and make every minute count. I wanted the viewing of our show to be a worthwhile experience for our viewers. What helped me relax was to imagine that I was speaking directly to my friends and relatives who I knew were watching.

On top of the news and the exercises, on that first program Dan and I interviewed four TV repairmen—Ben Benedict of American Television, Matt Legowik of Montgomery Ward, Dan Carter of TV Service Center and Jake Jones of Jones Westside TV—who discussed how to keep a television set in good working order. Our second interview was with Mrs. Harold Juedeman, with the League of Women Voters, who discussed the importance of women's involvement in politics.

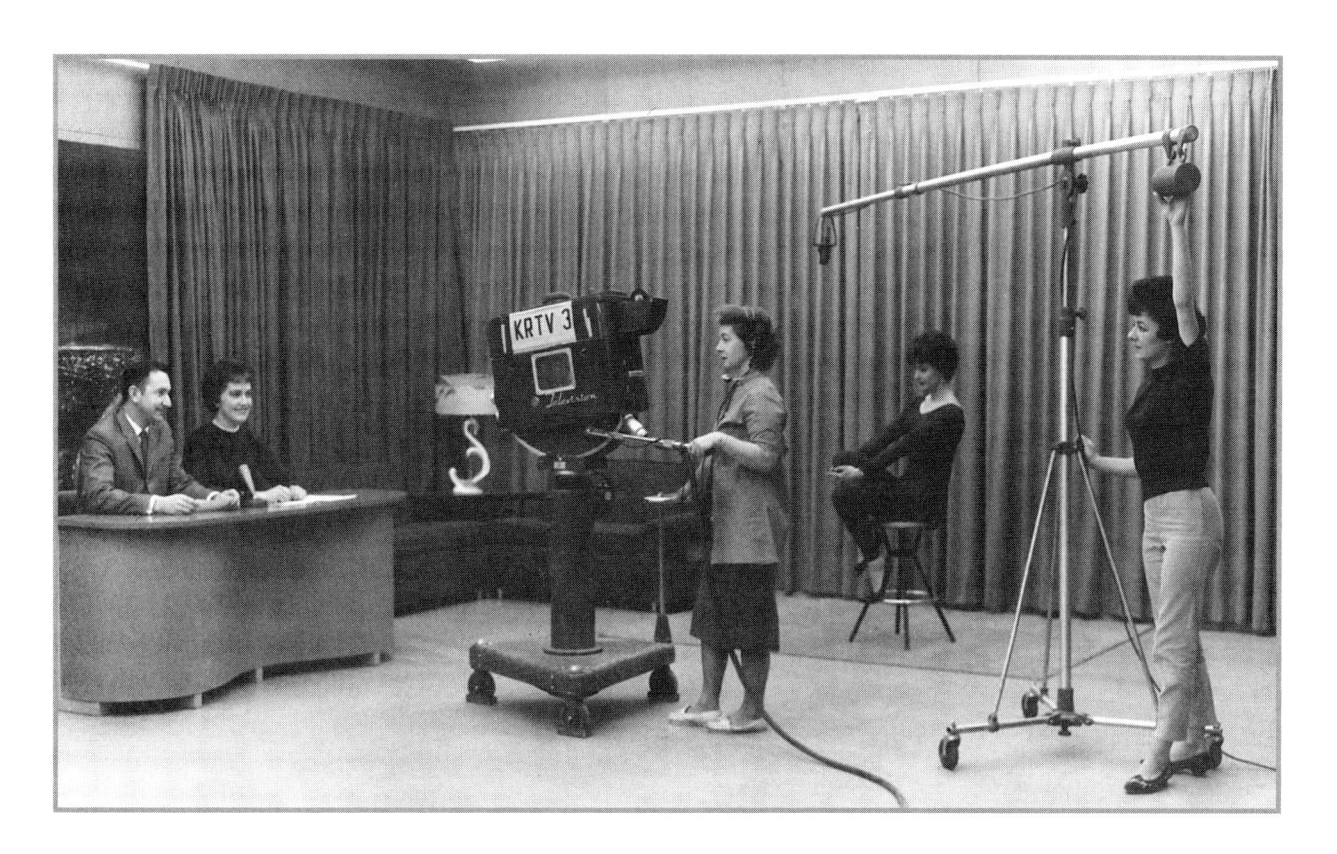

Dan introduced the new show with these words:

> Why are we taking off two morning quiz shows to bring you *Today in Montana*? We're taking them off not because we don't like them—it's kind of early in the morning to be playing games and people don't have enough time to follow these shows like they should. From 8 to 9, we feel that they need news and information and also we have had lots of requests to have an exercise program. Part of our program every day will be exercises.
>
> We have never had a program where we could have people sit down and talk to them and not be worried about the clock. We will feature interviews in depth.
>
> Some of our interviews will be with important people who come to our town. We hope to have the governor, and the mayor has agreed to make some regular appearances. We're going to have some people who will be discussing philosophy. We want to get into politics—we may have a Democrat and a Republican on at the same time and we'll ask them why they are members of their respective parties.
>
> Our program may get controversial, but we will remain

Today in Montana set and crew, with co-hosts Dan Snyder and Norma Beatty, camerawoman Edna Lockwood, exercise girl Barbara Taylor and boom mike operator Jeannie Hayden. DEMIER STUDIO

neutral. We hope to spotlight some of the good entertainment and what's going on in our schools.

The only film portion of the show will be a clinical psychologist, who is Dr. Joyce Brothers....We will also be featuring hairstyles, beauty tips and fashions every week.

We were off to a good start. With Dan's guidance, I had learned to ad-lib, and I learned the importance of timing. Following our daily format, which timed every segment to the minute, helped me to do that. The program ran in three different time slots for five days a week, 52 weeks a year for 24 years. The final two years of my career in KRTV, I did interviews on the *Noon News*, which is still on the air, and on *Perspective on Great Falls*, a public service program.

Norma Beatty's first business card from KRTV.

I learned another important lesson after being on the air only a few days. I was having a good time and I laughed a lot. Then I received several letters criticizing my laugh—one even said I made Dan laugh the way I did! One woman wrote saying the only reason she watched our show was because her radio was broken. I stopped laughing. Then letters arrived, asking me why I had stopped laughing. Was I sick?

I realized that I couldn't please everyone, so I would just be myself and do the best I could. I thought about their best censor, which was at the end of their arm. If people didn't like our show, they could always turn us off or switch to the other channel.

"We have never had a program where we could have people sit down and talk to them and not be worried about the clock."

As a woman on television, there were several challenges, including hair, wardrobe and makeup. KRTV never had a hairstylist, wardrobe mistress, or makeup artist, so these tasks were always mine. Rain or shine, I tried to look my best. Wigs and hairpieces came in handy at times. Hested's, a local department store, provided my wardrobe for a while. I would select five outfits at a time, so I could wear something different every day of the week. At the end of the show, the store got credit for my wardrobe. I always wore foundation, lipstick, blush, and mascara and powdered my shiny nose.

The other thing I always did was to take pictures. Some people do pottery, others make afghans. I do scrapbooks. On the first day of the show, Dan asked Great Falls photographer Andy DeMier to take photos of us in the studio. From that day forward, I had my own camera on hand and was able to take pictures of guests that I preserved in many scrapbooks—some of those photos are included in this book. I always kept show formats, letters, files, transcripts, audio tapes and videotapes. I have drawn on this material to help me remember the people and experiences I will treasure forever.

Interviewing

In the first few weeks on *Today in Montana*, Dan sat alongside me to help with the interviews. We quickly established good chemistry between us and took turns asking questions without interrupting each other.

Then on Tuesday, March 13, 1962, I had my trial by fire. Dan and I were talking to Ray Dodds, the championship basketball coach for the Great Falls High School Bison, when Dan suddenly got up and walked off the set. To this day I'm not exactly sure why he left. I was alone to talk to our guest.

The interview was scheduled for fifteen minutes, so the challenge before me was to finish it. I couldn't panic. I couldn't run, even though I was sorely tempted to. I had to muster up every tidbit of knowledge I had about basketball and ask some decent questions. Fortunately, I knew something about the game, so I asked him about his players, the kind of practice he put his players through, his defense strategy and his keys to having a winning team.

Ray was a good guest. He spoke eloquently about the sport and his championship team. When those fifteen minutes were over, I was drenched in sweat, relieved and happy. I had conducted my first solo interview on the air before 7,500 viewers.

Norma interviewing actors Audie Murphy and Susan Cabot, who co-starred in the film *Tumbleweeds* that premiered in Helena in 1953.

My first celebrity interview was in 1953, when I was on the staff of my school newspaper, *The Nugget,* at Helena High School. My guests were movie stars Susan Cabot and Audie Murphy, who was also the most decorated soldier of WWII. They were co-starring in a western *Tumbleweed,* that had premiered in Helena. Audie Murphy was 5'6," two inches shorter than I, so I spent most of my time with him trying to bend my knees so I wouldn't appear taller.

After working as a reporter three summers on the *Helena Independent Record* and receiving a journalism degree in 1957 from the University of Montana in Missoula, I knew the basics—the who, what, where, when, why and how of an interview. But interviewing people on live television was a very different experience. The advantages are that you can never misquote or misinterpret what a guest says—what they say is what they say. Also the spontaneity of a live interview can be a wonderful thing, especially when a guest says something totally unexpected. And, because television is a visual medium, you can show as well as tell the audience about the subject.

There are also obvious disadvantages to live interviews. You have no time to edit what is said. You do not have the luxury of talking about many things because your time is restricted: you must go on the air when the camera operator gives you the signal; you must go off the air when your time is up. You have to stick to the subject. If your guest freezes, you need to fill in until your time segment is over.

Norma and Art Linkletter, speaker for the Junior League Celebrity Series in 1976.

Dan Snyder gave me helpful tips about being a good interviewer. He suggested that I keep my questions short and to the point and to ask questions that prompt a good answer, instead of just a "yes" or "no." He reminded me to let the guest do most of the talking—all the while reminding them of the time restrictions—because I was on the air every day, the guest was not. It was important, he emphasized, to be prepared for your guest. If it was an author, I was to have an idea what his or her book was about; if it was an actor, I was to familiarize myself with his or her career. His final tip was to keep myself focused in the interview—to know what I wanted to cover and then to do it.

I also gained valuable advice from Art Linkletter, who probably interviewed more children than anyone through his TV show *Kids*

Say the Darndest Things. He said to be a good conversationalist, "Be genuinely interested in the person. Listen intently and answer and participate. Because if you can't participate it's just a one way conversation. But listening is most important."

Audrey Creecy had her own show, *Woman's World,* and later *The Audrey Show* opposite me on KFBB from 1967 to 1977, and we had fun appearing on one another's shows. First we reminded our viewers who was whom—we were often mistaken for one another. Then we provided these do's and don'ts for being interviewed on television:

1. Don't wear black or white, stripes or checks. Pastels and solid colors look best.
2. Do wear a cowboy hat placed toward the back of the head, otherwise your face will be in the dark.
3. Don't wear clanky chains. The noise will be picked up on the microphone. Bright shiny jewelry also reflects the lights in the studio.
4. Don't look at yourself on the monitor.
5. Do work out your movements with the camera when you are holding up an object to be seen by the television viewers. If you hold an item up too quickly, the camera will have difficulty following you.

Features

Before long, I added features to *Today in Montana*—a song of the day, a hymn of the week, a joke of the day, a thought for the day, a Montana historical fact, a monthly book review, a movie review, a fish and game report, a poem of the week, health report, and a monthly birthday box drawing. We also carried "NBC News with Nancy Dickerson."

A number of these features required that we develop a *Today in Montana* family. Among our early regular members was Glenn Lockwood, who covered news, weather and the poem of the week.

In addition to providing news and weather, George Tilton was a co-host. Joan Mora took over for Barbara Taylor with exercises, such as sit-ups, leg lifts and stretches. Lou Bryant played the song of the day with his accordion—songs ranging from "Accordiana" to "Flight of the Bumble Bee." Tony Pinski provided the hymn of the week— "The Lord's Prayer" was his favorite—accompanied by Lou.

Others who made regular appearances were Betty Furdell and Etheljean Forsman with book reviews. Roger Fliger gave the fish

Audie Murphy was 5'6," two inches shorter than I, so I spent most of my time with him trying to bend my knees so I wouldn't appear taller.

CRAIG WIRTH, who went on to have an illustrious television career in Los Angeles, New York and Salt Lake City, had this unexpected meeting with Svetlana Starodomskaya, a broadcaster from Moscow, Russia, whom I had interviewed for *Today in Montana*. Here is the letter he wrote me:

It comes on a cold night in April of 1990. It was one of the loneliest nights of my life as I was working my third or fourth night in Moscow. At the time, Western journalists were not really welcomed and tended to have to move around. I had been shuffled to a four-story cement structure surrounded by a hundred other four-story cement structures—somewhere an hour from Red Square. I had no idea where I was. But ironically, I thought there are about 250 missiles in Montana that know where I am as they are all aimed at me this cold night in Moscow.

A producer from Minnesota had arranged for me to spend the night on the floor of a flat next to a Russian journalist's apartment. However, I would have to make necessary arrangements with the Russian journalist who was not at home. I had to sneak up a freight lift....

I was let into the two-room flat of the Russian journalist. I quietly sat across from an elderly lady from the Ukraine who was the journalist's mother....Her daughter the journalist arrived. Svetlana Starodomskaya was like the aunt all of us loved in our childhood. She was bubbly, warm, and made me ashamed I had grown up learning that I must hate Russians. After all, thirty years prior, I had sat in East Junior High hearing the Malmstrom radar dish "Big Bertha" send a chirp into the Junior High speakers in every room as it powerfully searched for Russians who were out to get us.

Svetlana had little in her apartment in the line of decorations. She had bookcases crowded with life's possessions, and a little kitchen where she fried two pieces of cheese. That seemed to be her only fresh food that day. She shared a generous portion with me. We didn't know what to say. I looked up to one wall by a bookcase, and there was a big yellow button what one would pin to a shirt. Even though the electricity failed to produce much light, I could read it by memory. That is because this big yellow button and many more like it were handed out by one bundle of energy who started my career that led to this night...The button clearly said, "I'm from Montana." I pointed at it and said my first words, "Norma Ashby."

She stood up and screamed "Norma! Ashby!" Her elderly mother, who spoke no English, watched in amazement. Svetlana and I embraced as she grabbed my arm and led me to an old desk....She pulled out a scrapbook and showed me notes and letters from Norma Ashby....

We talked all night. All the buttons Norma handed out...all the pictures Norma Ashby took..all the scrapbooks. One name made two journalists who didn't know what to say, talk volumes. One name made two people from half way around the world realize people are just people....I no longer fear the art of conversation as the common person's embrace. And I look at a map of the former Soviet Union, a land that I had been taught to hate, and remember when for one night it was home, really home. All because of Norma Ashby.

I have been very lucky in my career. I have Emmy Awards and lots of tapes of lucky breaks. I have plastered my office walls with pictures of me reporting from the Berlin Wall, reporting from an old battlefield in North Carolina, with the bus that took me around America for my prime time cable show, and a picture of me and Linda Ellerbee, when I was on her show. But in my house, in the area I keep for cherished people, I have a picture of Norma Ashby, George Tilton and me at the old desk of *Today in Montana*. That is because all the other pictures from my career come as a result of that one year when I learned the passion of television—the year of *Today* in Montana.

and game report, often bringing live animals into the studio. Zella Jacobson, a nurse, conducted a question-and-answer session with a studio audience and a guest. Carl Kochman, Chris Hoy, Joe Lawson and Tim Luinstra—all avid movie-goers— provided movie reviews; and Leona Bergmann gave gardening tips and introduced the flower of the month by describing the flower's characteristics.

Still others who were part of the show during the ten-year period *Today in Montana* was a local program included: Helen Huntsberger, Babe Young, J.C. Johnson, Lisette Bennett, Lynn Compton, Tug Ikeda, Mary Ellen Lucken, Eileen Solberg and Nita Wolf, who took turns doing the exercise segment. Craig Wirth, a Great Falls high school junior who went on to have an illustrious television career in Salt Lake City, Los Angeles and New York, did a weekly commentary called "Craig's Corner," which he wrote himself. One featured a hilarious anecdote from an old newspaper he found in his grandmother's attic.

Don Bradley and Marty Wilcox offered news and weather. Bob Deming, John Pearson and June Meier—who all worked at the Montana School for the Deaf and the Blind in Great Falls—signed news for our deaf viewers, which was quite a progressive addition for the times. Elizabeth Love and Richard Gercken gave library reports, Jim Poor spoke about art, LeRoy Stahl talked about school news, Marge Elerding covered travel, and Nancy Stephenson, the Junior League. Book reviews were given by Chris Stevens, Sam Dachs and Dan Cushman. The flower of the month was covered by Lucille White and Helen Trebesch.

ABOVE: Craig Wirth in 1985, when he was a feature reporter with WOR-TV in New York City. Craig had a feature, "Craig's Corner," on *Today in Montana* when he was a high school student in Great Falls.

BELOW: Norma with Russian journalist Svetlana Starodomskaya on *Today in Montana* in May 1977.

When you work together so closely with people doing a show, you become close. Working with all of these people who were in front of the camera was an enriching experience for me. We were an extended family and good friends. We had birthday parties for each other. We laughed and cried together. We watched our children grow up. Some of us still get together for an annual reunion.

Behind the camera, we also had an exceptional crew. Foremost was our director Larry Millard who kept the show on schedule during my entire career at KRTV. He had the perfect disposition for what could have been a nerve-wracking job. He always kept his cool. When I asked Larry what he liked about the show, he said, "You were the best interviewer I ever worked with, but I was pretty good at what I did, too. I always protected your guests and I always protected you from embarrassment. I tried to put our best face forward. That's why your show was so good."

Our studio cameramen and women included Wayne Schultz, Edna Lockwood, Jeannie Hayden, Susie Rothenbuehler, Marilyn and Larry McDaniel, Walt Mann, Marliss Urton, Shirley Hunt and Shari Pullar.

One day Shari told me she was a witch and said she could prove it. We wanted to put a *Today in Montana* T-shirt on a live rooster to shoot a promo for the show. Shari put her hand on the beak of the rooster and moved it back and forth, hypnotizing it. It worked! The rooster plopped over on the table and she was able to put the T-shirt on it. Then she snapped her fingers. The rooster stood up and we filmed him for the promo. He made a perfect model. I still have the rooster's T-shirt among my TV memorabilia.

The rooster who was hypnotized by camerawoman Shari Pullar in 1981 for a special promotion.

pk..pk..pk **pkaw!**

We had a great deal of viewer participation in the show. We had a monthly birthday box, where people would send in the names of friends and family, and we received dozens of entries. When a name was drawn, the winner would receive a bouquet of flowers from Feiden's Flowers and later the Electric City Conservatory. Sometimes I would personally deliver the flowers.

One winner was the husband of Mrs. Rdee Brown,

who lived on the west side of Great Falls. She and I took an instant liking to each other and we became close friends. We took turns treating each other to lunch every month for more than fifteen years until she died in 2002 at the age of ninety-six. She was a dear person and I am blessed to have had her in my life. She became my adopted mother after my mother's death and I became her adopted daughter after her daughter's death.

Jokes, thoughts and poems were also supplied in abundance by the viewers, which I would use and credit the sender. Here is the most requested poem. With his deep, resonant voice, Glenn Lockwood read this poem by Toni Knudson of Highwood, Montana.

Trail's End Ranch

There's a mighty heap of living
Away out here on the farm.
Where the day that ends at sunset
Begins at the break of dawn.

Where the stillness is so peaceful
I can hear the pheasants cry
And watch some deer in the shelter belt
And the jet trails in the sky.

Where the summer days are busy
But I still find time to go
To pick the pasture's wildflowers
And see where the chokecherries grow.

Where the winter days are white and clean
And tracks lead everywhere
And I can do as I very well please
Free from summer's care.

Oh I have been to Waikiki
Seen the Sphinx and Taj Mahal
Moonlight on the Ganges
And the Empire State so tall.

I've sailed through the streets of Venice
Toured the ruins of ancient Rome

Shari put her hand on the beak of the rooster and moved it back and forth, hypnotizing it. It worked! The rooster plopped over on the table and she was able to put the T-shirt on it. Then she snapped her fingers. The rooster stood up and we filmed him for the promo.

Yes I've found time to enjoy them all
Curled up with my books at home.

I'll live my life in this valley
Overlooking the river breaks
And I'll not envy the traveler
World-weary from the trips he makes.

For there's a mighty heap of living
In this land we love so well
If we learn to live with what we have
No matter where we dwell.

News

During my twenty-six years at KRTV, I was privileged to work with experienced staff members who did the evening news.

Gene Marianetti was one of our earliest prime time news readers. He also did news at KMON radio, so, he did double service. This was before film and videotape. He went on to have an outstanding career in public affairs with the NASA space program in Washington, D. C.

Bill Whitsitt was our news director from 1966-1970. From 1970 to 1971 he took a year off to be a CBS News Fellow, studying political science and American government in the graduate program at Columbia University in New York City.

He came back from 1972-1973 and created the Montana Television Network news organization.

One of my favorite stories about Bill is when he was doing the weather live during a party at the station. Several of us girls decided to see if we could "break him up" on the air. We individually gave him a kiss on the cheek and he never batted an eye. We will never forget his composure in what could have been a very trying situation.

Bill went on to careers in government, education and government relations in Washington, D. C. We still keep in touch and are good friends.

Ed Coghlan was at KRTV from 1969-1984. He was 19 years old and a sophomore at the College of Great Falls when he was hired as an intern by Bill Whitsitt to work twenty hours a week. He did farm news and sports.

In 1976 he was hired by Joe Sample and Don Bradley to be news director of the Montana Television Network. He said their support was "incredible."

Ed listed special achievements during his years at KRTV: Election nights, and pushing to get state basketball tournaments on the air. Asked how he handled criticism, Ed said, "I was young, aggressive and Irish."

Ed left KRTV in 1984 to become news director at KCOP-TV in Los Angeles, a major career move from a small market to one of the major markets in the country. I interviewed him four years later when he and his wife Diane and their five children came home for a celebration of her father's birthday in Butte.

I asked Ed about highlights of his TV career in Los Angeles.

He said they were the Olympics; the Pope's visit, which was a big undertaking with all the TV stations pooling their coverage; the earthquake; and the Los Angeles marathon, which required twenty-eight cameras.

Looking back at his time at KRTV, Ed said, "It was the highlight of my life to be MTN news director. We were unique in the nation. When I got to Los Angeles, I realized how good we had been."

Referring to the connections he had made with viewers here, he

1967 cast of *Today in Montana* (from left): Glenn Lockwood, news; Joan Mora, exercises; Dan Snyder and Norma Ashby, co-hosts; Tony Pinski, hymn of the week; and Lou Bryant, song of the day.

said, "I'll never forget when we left. I was getting letters from people that caused tears to well up in my eyes. 'You have been part of my life,' they wrote. 'We have watched you grow up.' You get a unique feel about the people you work for in a market this size." After his career in broadcasting, Ed was in the medical device and medical technology field in California and Colorado. He is now working with a political consulting firm in California.

Hospitality Time

I also assisted Maxine Otis, the home service advisor for the Great Falls Gas Company, on her biweekly cooking show, *Hospitality Time,* that immediately followed *Today in Montana* from 9 to 9:30 a.m.

We had a kitchen set up in the studio and Maxine prepared dishes on the air. We offered the recipes to our viewers and the response was overwhelming.

The Great Falls Gas Company published a cookbook featuring 185 of the favorite recipes demonstrated on *Hospitality Time*, which was broadcast on KRTV for more than six years. It was the longest-running television program in Montana at the time with a single sponsor.

Of all the recipes Maxine shared, my favorite from her cookbook, long out of print, is Chinese Hot Dish. The dish has become a tradition in our family. We serve it regularly, especially on Christmas Eve.

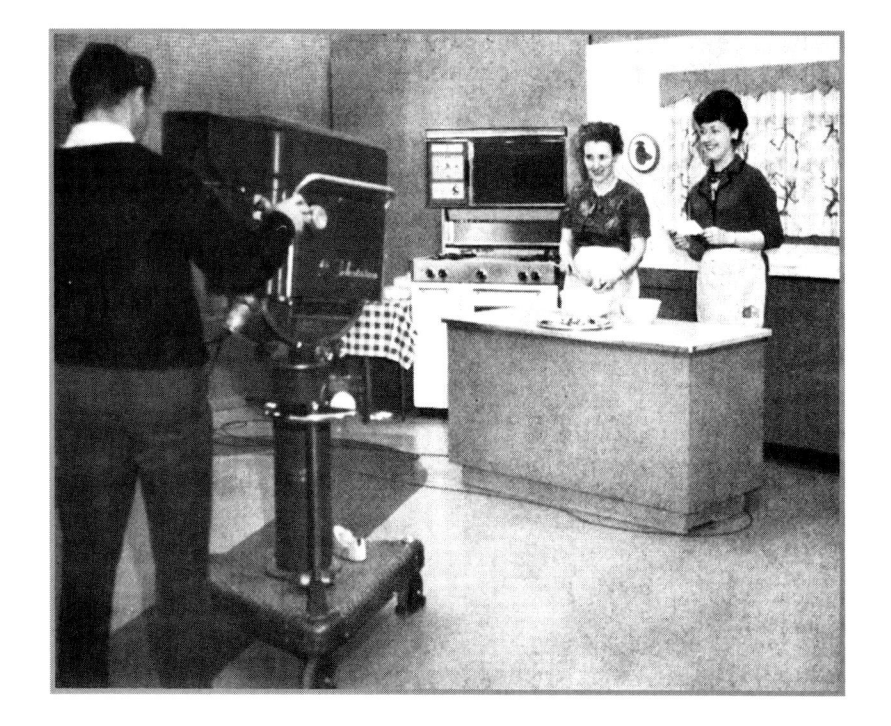

Maxine Otis, home service advisor for the Great Falls Gas Company and Norma on the *Hospitality Time* cooking show that ran twice a week for six years. John Hildenstab was cameraman.

Advertisers

Along with featuring live interviews, *Today in Montana* sported a number of advertisements by merchants who did their own spots live on the air. They did not have to pay extra for this and they did not have to take a screen test. They just came to the studio with their merchandise and did them. These included Wally's Superette, a neighborhood grocery store, whose spokesman was John Stanish. He would carefully arrange large displays of meat on a table and talk about

CHINESE HOT DISH

1 lb. ground beef or 1 lb. cubed veal or venison	1 can chicken rice soup
	1 can water
2 Tbs. fat	4.Tbs. soy sauce
1 cup finely choped onion	1 cup finely diced celery
½ cup washed uncooked rice	1 pkg. frozen peas

Brown meat in fat; add chopped onion and cook until golden and transparent. Add rice, soup, water and soy sauce. Place in 2 quart covered casserole and bake in 400° gas oven for 1 hour. During the last twenty minutes, add 1 cup finely diced celery and 1 pkg. frozen peas. More liquid may be needed.

---

the "best buys of the week." The memorable thing about his spots was that he had to keep batting away the flies that found the meat appealing.

Ingrid Crymes, the "Hat Lady," did live spots for her hat department at The Paris, a large department store in Great Falls. She would talk about and show the latest styles that no lady would want to be without. Occasionally she would use me for a model, which I always enjoyed. She also sold wigs. Both hats and wigs were very popular in the 1960s and 1970s and she did a great job promoting them.

Evelyn Weismann, from the the Viking Shop, a gift store in the 1100 block on Central Avenue, was our most faithful advertiser. She called us the second day the show was on the air and said she wanted to be a part of *Today in Montana*. She would bring a selection of beautiful gift items such as Royal Copenhagen figurines, Orefors crystal and Madame Alexander dolls to the studio, display them and talk about them. Rita Miller (later Ginter), her assistant, Miller did a great job selling merchandise on the show, too.

Advertising rates for the show were modest by today's standards. A 1968 rate card showed a 60-second spot cost $12.50. A 60-second spot in that time slot today would be $50.

There were also faithful sponsors of our special features. Hempl's Bakery provided beautifully decorated sheet cakes big enough to serve our entire crew and studio guests. Feiden's Flowers and later the Electric City Conservatory furnished flower arrangements to highlight our monthly birthday box drawings.

Family Christmas Shows

One of the delights of being on *Today in Montana* was our annual Christmas show, which featured staff members and their families.

Norma's favorite recipe from the Hospitality Time show, which she makes every year for Christmas Eve.

ABOVE: The *Today in Montana* family Christmas show in 1972. First row, from left: Joan Mora, Lou Bryant and Dan Tilton. Second row: Steve Roth (Norma's nephew), Norma, Joanne Mora, Scott Tilton, Loren Pinski, Richard "Klem" Klemencic as Santa Claus, Laurie Tilton, Jerri Mora, George Tilton and Tony Pinski.

FACING PAGE: The cover of the 1969 *TV/Radio Mirror* that featured an article about Norma and *Today in Montana*.

On December 24, 1968, for example, we featured co-host George Tilton and his three children, Scott, Dan and Laurie, whom George talked to about Christmas. Newscaster Glenn Lockwood appeared with his two-year-old granddaughter, Cory. Joan Mora and two of her daughters, Jerri and Joanne, helped her do exercises; Tony Pinski and his son Loren sang a song together. My ten-year-old nephew, Steve Roth, appeared with me. He sang "A Place in the Sun" accompanied by guitarist Bill Cane. The song was a poem I had written, which Steve had put to music and Jack Harper had arranged.

The highlight of this show was always our special guest, Santa Claus, portrayed for many years by Richard "Klem" Klemencic. He was a jolly, rotund man who made the perfect Santa. He would talk to me about the favorite toys he was making for children, Mrs. Santa, whom he called "Mama," and his reindeer. He then would ask each of the children what they wanted for Christmas and always reminded them to leave some milk and chocolate chip cookies for him. We would conclude the program by singing together, "We Wish You a Merry Christmas."

Dan Snyder Sells KRTV

A major change occurred at KRTV and on the *Today in Montana* show when Dan Snyder sold KRTV in 1968 to Joe Sample, a broadcast executive from Billings, for $1,000,000. It was an adjustment for the staff since we were a closely knit group used to having the owner under our roof. Others ably stepped into Dan's place on the show, including George Tilton and Glenn Lockwood, who served the most years by my side as host. Joe Sample proved to be a visionary who created the Montana Television Network and who was responsible for *Today in Montana* going statewide.

Dan continued in broadcasting serving stations in Billings and Helena and is now Kalispell sales rep for radio stations KERR and

KQRK-FM in Polson and working with sales for a new radio station, KIBG in Bigfork. His broadcasting career spans fifty-six years, since his college days at the University of Montana in 1948. I have continued to keep in touch with Dan and am indebted to him for writing the forward to this book. He has influenced many lives in broadcasting including mine.

Today in Montana Goes Statewide

After ten and a half years as a successful local television show, KRTV's *Today in Montana* show in Great Falls became a statewide program on the Montana Television Network on August 21, 1972. It became a half-hour show that appeared weekday mornings from 9:00 to 9:30 a.m. Now, instead of being seen in just the Great Falls area, *Today in Montana* was also seen on KTVQ in Billings, KXLF in Butte and KPAX in Missoula.

In addition to our show, the newscast originating from KRTV went statewide that same year. Joe Sample acquired the first of his four stations, KOOK-TV, now KTVQ in Billings in 1957. In 1961 he bought KXLF-TV in Butte and KRTV in 1968. He started a satellite station in Missoula, KPAX, in 1970 and built it into a full-fledged broadcast operation in 1977. He said he believed that the statewide newscast and *Today in Montana* show might help bridge the state's vast geographic barriers separating Montanans. If Billings viewers, for example, could watch important stories and interviews from Great Falls, Missoula and Butte as well, he believed Montanans might be able to resolve some of the major political and social issues without some of the rancor that has characterized the state's history.

The result of several top level meetings between staff members of all participating stations, the new statewide *Today in Montana* show originated live from the studios of KRTV. With input from station managers, reporters and those who became editors for the show at each station, we redesigned the format and developed new sets to give the show a new look.

The program consisted of a brief opening, five minutes of Montana news and weather—including film reports done by the MTN news staff. There was a statewide segment, varying in length from seven to ten minutes, featuring interviews, special reports and several regular features such as cooking and book reviews, and a local five minute segment which enabled each station to satisfy its public service requests. Four commercial breaks were scheduled during the thirty minutes. This format lasted for fourteen years.

The program highlights from that first year included a feature on First Lady Pat Nixon's visit to Yellowstone National Park on its centennial, a trip on the Milk River Wagon train near Malta, a history of the Montana State Prison with Deputy Warden Jim Blodgett, as well as a piece on the Yellowstone Boys Ranch in Billings. We had notables such as Democrat Tom Judge and Republican Ed Smith, who were candidates for the governor's office, and Mayors John McLaughlin of Great Falls, Mike Micone of Butte and Willard Fraser of Billings. U. S. Senate candidates and their wives, including incumbent Democratic Senator Lee Metcalf and his wife Donna, and Republican challenger Henry Hibbard and his wife Jane, discussed their personal lives and what they liked and didn't like about campaigning. We had country western singer Charley Pride, as well as Stan Lynde, creator of the comic strip, *Rick O'Shay*.

Our first statewide rating indicated that in the short time we had been on the air, we were building strong audiences in the new areas

Norma and cartoonist Stan Lynde holding up a sample of his *Rick O'Shay* comic strip in 1972.

we were reaching and increasing our audience in north central Montana.

As the producer and hostess of the new statewide show, I was pleased to have the endorsement of the management and the cooperation of the MTN stations in order to make this new concept in Montana broadcasting happen.

KRTV's New Home

Another landmark event happened in 1972. The staff of KRTV moved into a new one-million-dollar building west of the former building on the old Havre highway. Designed by PageWerner Architects of Great Falls, Joe Sample had requested that the building make a significant architectural contribution to the City of Great Falls. Its four octagonal shaped pods were built of steel. General Manager Cliff Ewing said other broadcasters from around the country told him it was the most unique TV station building they had ever seen.

In 1981, Joe Sample commissioned Lyndon Pomeroy, a Billings artist, to create a sculpture to be placed in front of the building. He did a metal sculpture of an Indian, standing on top of a horse, holding a mirror in his hands. This symbolized the first communication on the prairie as the sunlight would reflect off the glass to another Indian miles away. A contest was held for its name, and *"Suntalker"* was chosen.

The *Today in Montana* cast in 1969 in costumes representing the past, present and future. From left: Glenn Lockwood, inspirational readings; Joan Mora, exercises; Lou Bryant, musician; Tony Pinski, songs; Norma, hostess and producer; and George Tilton, host.

Anniversaries

The tenth anniversary of *Today in Montana* on February 18, 1972, was special to me because it was the last anniversary show we would celebrate as a local program in north central Montana. That August, we would go statewide and take on a whole new dimension.

Dan Snyder opened the show with me and gave this answer when I asked him why he decided to put a show like *Today in Montana* on KRTV:

> At that particular time there wasn't any such show. I felt the community and this part of Montana needed a local expression where local people could be on television and

express themselves...where we could do something different.

So I found this girl by the name of Norma Beatty at that particular time and I asked her if she would be interested. She took everything in hand and really did a great job. After ten years as the same hostess and the same gal, I just think it's wonderful.

Dan and I blew out ten candles on a large decorated sheet cake donated by Hempl's Bakery. We shared highlights of the program's first decade, including the live fire on the set. A hot studio light had gotten too close to a curtain and caused it to catch fire. Dan told me to keep talking while he put out the fire with a fire extinguisher.

We showed a picture of our black and white studio camera that Dan said cost $600. Our first studio color camera, which the station bought in 1967, cost $80,000. When we finally did go to color, Dan gave me two blouses to wear on the show—one orange and the other aqua. I still have the blouses!

Former Miss Montana Joanna Lester Sievers of Helena sang our theme song, "I Ain't Down Yet;" Tom Harwood and his oldtime fiddlers from Valier performed; Tony Pinski sang "Great Day," accompanied by Lou Bryant on accordion; and the College of Great Falls Chansoniers, under the direction of Lee Matthews, sang a medley of songs.

We offered gift drawings for a wide variety of gifts provided by sponsors, from bubble bath to an Eva Gabor wiglet, and the response from viewers was huge. We received 810 cards and letters from viewers in sixty-four Montana towns and two Canadian towns.

We received telegrams, letters and birthday cards. These are a few of the special ones we received:

Norma with flowers, letters and cards on the tenth anniversary show on February 19, 1972.

Mike Mansfield, Democratic senator from Montana and the Majority Leader of the U.S. Senate sent these congratulations:

> Congratulations to Station KRTV on the occasion of the Tenth Anniversary of Montana's longest running daily special television show, *Today in Montana*.
>
> Norma, since the inception of this program, you have done an outstanding job in bringing to the people of Montana a truly fine interview show.
>
> This locally produced program has brought to the viewers in-depth interviews with personalities of state, nation-wide and international fame.
>
> I wish you continued success and my personal regards to all at Station KRTV on this tenth Anniversary.

Cartoonist Stan Lynde sent a note saying that "Norma and *Today in Montana* just have to be two of Montana's finest resources."

A group of students from Fort Benton sent a handmade birthday card on which they wrote: "We were on the show once. We loved it! So did our school! So did our mothers!!" Also from Fort Benton, fifty students signed a twenty-foot-long banner wishing *Today in Montana* a happy tenth birthday.

Since tin is the metal for a tenth anniversary, I presented tin can trophies, created by Betty Magner, to each of the men I had worked with: Dan Snyder, George Tilton, Glenn Lockwood, Lou Bryant and Tony Pinski. Glenn then surprised me with gifts also created in tin by Betty Magner, from the staff of KRTV. These were: a star that signified KRTV's *Today in Montana* show that would soon reach all points in Montana, a chair representing my hostess chair, a glass signifying a toast to Dan, Glenn, Lou, George, Tony and me and all the past and present friends who had made our show such a success.

At the conclusion of the show I visited with my dear mother, Ella Mehmke. She congratulated me on the show's anniversary and said she hoped she would be with me for the show's twentieth birthday. Her words were prophetic. She died of cancer nine years

Vocalist Tony Pinski and musician Lou Bryant on the tenth anniversary of *Today in Montana* on February 19, 1972

Senator Lee Metcalf and Norma in 1973.

A picture from the set of the fifteenth anniversary show on February 19, 1977. From left: Norma's mother, Ella Mehmke; Evelyn Weismann of the Viking Shop, winner of the Most Loyal Sponsor Award; Norma; and Alice Tintinger, winner of the Most Loyal Viewer Award.

later in 1981 at the age of seventy-six. Her happy spirit remains with me to this day.

On the occasion of our fifteenth anniversary on February 19, 1977, these greetings were noteworthy:

From Senator Lee Metcalf and his wife Donna:

Dear Norma,
The fifteenth Anniversary of *Today in Montana* is a landmark for Montana television and a personal triumph for you.

Donna and I, who have known you ever since you were a Blue Bird in Donna's group when we lived in Helena, and I was on the Supreme Court, have watched your achievements with pride.

Donna says that you gave indications of your future attainments when you were the most innovative and talkative of a group of girls, all of whom were quite special.

From Governor Tom Judge:

I would like to take this opportunity to extend my best wishes and congratulations from Carol and myself to Norma Ashby and *Today in Montana*, which is celebrating its fifteenth anniversary this week.

Fifteen years ago *Today in Montana* went on the air as strictly a local show. Today it is statewide. We have enjoyed watching the numerous interviews of Montanans about the exciting things they are doing in this state and in many fields of endeavor. And also the famous people from the arts, from politics, from science and business and industry that have come to our state and have been interviewed on this program.

I would like to join with thousands of Montanans and extend our best wishes to Norma Ashby and the future of *Today in Montana*, the only program of its kind in the State of Montana.

From Joe Sample, president of the Montana Television Network:

> For those of you in the Great Falls area, this is the fifteeth anniversary of *Today in Montana*. In other parts of the state it is only the fifth year in which it has been available through the facilities of the Montana Television Network.
>
> Good program ideas are very rare. They just don't grow on trees. We felt that KRTV and Norma Ashby had an exceptional idea. So five years ago we extended the program to the full network. We are very pleased with the results. The acceptance in Butte, Billings, and Missoula has been every bit as great as it was in Great Falls.
>
> We look forward to many more years of *Today in Montana* at an even higher level than it is today.

Our twentieth anniversary was on February 19, 1982 at KRTV before a studio audience of sixty-five guests. We received cards and

This watercolor by Bob Morgan was given to Norma to commemorate the twentieth anniversary of the show. In the painting, Bob portrays historical characters that might have appeared on the show.

letters from 3,000 viewers in 205 Montana, Wyoming and Canadian towns, who entered the prize drawings for such gifts as a weekend for two in Yellowstone National Park and a Yogo sapphire pendant. It was exciting to see the names and geographical diversity of the Montana communities ranging from Absarokee to Zurick, from Cardwell to Walkerville.

In addition to roses and an orchid corsage, I was given gifts including a three-tiered handmade table from one of our former exercise leaders, Tug Ikeda; an original watercolor featuring Montana characters by Bob Morgan and an engraved gold pendant from my husband, Shirley Ashby.

Greetings poured in from everywhere. Taped greetings came from David Hartman, *Good Morning America*, Charley Pride, Bobby Burgess, Governor Ted Schwinden and A. B. "Bud" Guthrie. Sister MTN stations sent their greetings.

We received dozens of tributes, from people ranging from Willard Scott on the *Today Show* to my next door neighbor from Helena. This one from Dr. Bob Lind, human development specialist at MSU in Bozeman and a dear friend, was among my favorites.

Author A.B. "Bud" Guthrie promoting his book *Wild Pitch* in 1973.

To Norma:
It is well and wisely said
That where one's abilities and the needs of the world
Come to an intersection,
That is where you are called of God to serve.
The place where your abilities, Norma,
And the needs of Montana's people
Intersect is in that distance
Between the television set and the viewer's heart.
One could not do what you have done
Two hundred sixty times a year for twenty years
If it were only a job. It has to be a calling
That draws forth from you such deep compassion and caring.
Thousands of us have seen you off-camera,
And have realized you don't do a television act.
You really are in person what you seem to be on the screen.

Your attitudes of joy and wonder,
sensitivity and socialconcern are honest.
There are many thousands of us who
know you and feel close to you,
Even though we know you have not
personally met all of us.
It happens somehow, when the spirit
is right,
That geographic distances and personal introductions don't matter.
We are grateful for all you have
shown us and shared with us
These past twenty years. Great people, great ideas, interesting people,
Challenging thoughts, inspiration
and hope, have been daily fare.
That the program has achieved
such length is testimony to its
breadth and depth.
On the twentieth anniversary of
Today in Montana we do not wish
Merely to congratulate you, but to
thank you and to thank God for you.
For you to have lived your calling in our midst has
enriched us all.
You're very special—one of a kind—and we are grateful!

Dan Snyder, Norma and Glenn Lockwood on *Today in Montana*'s twentieth anniversary show at KRTV on February 19, 1982.

In the course of the program I visited with Dan Snyder, original host, and Glenn Lockwood, current host, and former featured musicians Lou Bryant and Tony Pinski. I honored our most loyal sponsor, the Viking Shop, which had been on the air since our second program, and gave a plaque to owner Evelyn Weismann and Rita Ginter, who did live commercials featuring their beautiful gift items.

I also honored our most loyal viewer in a special taped presentation. She was Alice Tintinger from Cascade, who had watched the show faithfully since it first went on the air.

Twenty-five Years in Broadcasting

My twenty-fifth anniversary in broadcasting was celebrated on February 19, 1987. Dan Snyder joined me on the program and we recalled our early years together on the air. By then KRTV had been sold two more times. George Lilly, a broadcast executive from Ithaca, New York, bought it as part of the Montana Television Network from Joe Sample in 1984 for $20 million and the show was moved from 9 a.m. to noon. Major changes were made in its format, lengthening the news and weather segments, adding an agriculture report and cutting the length of the statewide and local segments. I was still serving as producer and hostess. Then, in 1986, George Lilly sold KRTV, KPAX and KXLF to Evening Post Publishing Company in Charleston, South Carolina, for $24 million (Evening Post bought KTVQ in 1994 and today the Montana Television Network remains the only statewide television network in Montana) and the name of our show was changed to the *Noon News*. The program became primarily a news program and the interviews, which I still did at KRTV, were shortened. The show was anchored from KTVQ in Billings. I also became special projects director at KRTV and did regular weekly interviews on a thirty minute public affairs program, *Perspective on Great Falls*. It was the end of *Today in Montana* as we had known it.

Denise Mort, a reporter for the *Great Falls Tribune*, wrote a two page story about my "quarter century at home in front of camera" published along with eight photographs in the *Great Falls Tribune* "Preview" section for February 15, 1987. Among the many stories in the article was my interview with Colonel Joe Montgomery of Lewistown, a colorful character, who told me before he died in 1984 at the age of 107, that in his early years, he ran a string of whorehouses in the mining camps of Kendall and Maiden. This information was deemed "too raunchy" for use on television at the time, so we didn't air the interview—laughable when I think about the things that are commonly mentioned on television today.

TV Guide advertisement for *Today in Montana* in the 1970s.

I received flowers and many cards and letters from faithful viewers. Among them were: J. D. Holmes, who was my next door neighbor when I was growing up on Ninth Avenue in Helena and whom I credit with inspiring me to pursue a career in journalism—wrote "I begin to think that because you sometimes credit me for starting you on a news career that you also plan to equal my thirty years with one news agency (Associated Press). That would remove my only claim to fame—except that I've seen your appendicitis scar. "How many newsmen can brag about that?

This was a favorite accolade:

> City of Helena Proclamation
> Whereas, for twenty-five years Norma Beatty Ashby has enlightened and enriched the lives of Montanans through her *Today in Montana* program on KRTV, and
> Whereas, she makes the people of our great state feel like good friends as she covers with great geniality and good cheer everything from the birth of rattlesnakes to the death of political campaigns, and
> Whereas, she makes her state and its citizens feel proud of their accomplishments, and has emphasized the contributions made to Montana by its women, and
> Whereas, Norma Beatty Ashby is a native of Helena, (a fact we are very proud of) and a graduate of the University of Montana School of Journalism, and is involved in many activities promoting our great state.
> Now, Therefore, I, Russell J. Ritter, Mayor of the City of Helena, Montana, do hereby proclaim with great "Hometown Helena Pride," this Thursday,
> February 19, 1987, as NORMA BEATTY ASHBY DAY, in honor of her twenty-five years of outstanding service to the State of Montana.

My Bosses

I worked for four station managers and for four owners during my years at KRTV:

1962-1963, Paul Crain and Dan Snyder
1963-1968, Don Bradley and Dan Snyder
1969-1983, Cliff Ewing and Joe Sample
1984-1986, Pete Friden and George Lilly
1986-1988, Pete Friden and Evening Post Publishing Co.

After I left, Don Bradley served as general manager from 1988

When we finally did go to color, Dan gave me two blouses to wear on the show—one orange and the other aqua. I still have the blouses!

Shirley and Norma Ashby on their wedding day, September 5, 1964, at the First Presbyterian Church in Great Falls.

to 1994, and since then Bill Preston has been general manager. Evening Post continues as owner. They were all outstanding professionals in our field. Paul Crain, Pete Friden and Don Bradley are no longer with us.

Joys and Sorrows

In the course of my television career, I experienced some great personal joys as well as some great personal sorrows, all of which I shared with my viewers because of the nature of our show.

In 1962, I had been on the air only one month when my only sister, Annemarie Roth, died of cancer at the age of thirty-one. I had returned to Great Falls to be with her and I spent many precious hours at her bedside. She was a woman of deep faith. At one point I told her I was having a hard time understanding why God would take her when she had a husband and a three year old son and not me, a single woman. She said, "I have completed what God has sent me here to do. He is not finished with you yet. He has much more in store for you."

She died a short time after that conversation, but her simple reply has been a cornerstone of my life.

A few short months later, my step–brother, Jimmy Watson, who was in the Navy at the time, was killed at nineteen while he was hitchhiking in California—an unexpected tragedy eased only by the steady presence of friends and family.

Two years later, in February 1964, I met Shirley Ashby in Great Falls. As the agricultural liaison with Montana Bank, he had heard me give a speech about the Montana Territorial Centennial Celebration at a Foothills Livestock Association meeting in Eden. He had his thumb in a cast from a hunting accident and was too embarrassed to introduce himself. The day I met him, he was sitting two stools over from me at the counter at Schell's Restaurant and his cast had been removed.

He introduced himself and said, "I enjoyed your speech at Eden the other night."

Before I could reply he asked me if I liked to fly fish. I hadn't, but I had done some spin casting, so I said, "Yes."

He spent most of our courtship teaching me how to fly fish. I did everything wrong except catch more than he did.

This is his story about how we got engaged. He claims that after we had been going together a couple of weeks, he decided, why wait? You never really know anyone until you are married anyway. So he called me up one night and said, "Norma, would you like to get married?"

"Yes," I said. "Who is this?"

The truth of the matter is that we did have a whirlwind courtship, but it was three months, not two weeks long, and Shirley asked me to marry him in person, not on the phone.

We were married on September 5, 1964, in a large wedding at the First Presbyterian Church in Great Falls. My stepfather, Walter Mehmke, gave me away. When the preacher asked who gives this bride in marriage, Walter replied, "I do, her mother does, we all do."

Our viewers shared in the joy of this happy occasion with cards and letters, and I showed pictures of our wedding and honeymoon trip to Glacier Park, Banff and Lake Louise on *Today in Montana*.

Diplomat and playwright Clare Booth Luce once said, "A woman who has important responsibilities needs the right kind of man by her side." As the wife of Henry Luce, the founder and publisher of Time Magazine, she said, "A woman needs to love and to be loved, for a life without love is crippling at best and meaningless at worst."

I have been blessed to have a man like Shirley Ashby as my husband. Shirley has been my best cheerleader and my best critic. Throughout my public career I have never felt one bit of jealousy or resentment from him. I feel lucky to have him in my life. After all these years of fly fishing, I have gotten better, but he is still the best.

Several years later, in 1968, my late sister's ten-year-old son, Steve Roth, came to live with us for a year. He had been living with his father's parents in Yakima, Washington, and visiting us during the summers after Ann's death. Steve helped us become a family. This opened up a whole new world for us of Cub Scouts, parent-teacher conferences, and fun.

We are proud of Steve. He graduated from Harvard University

In the course of my television career, I experienced some great personal joys as well as some great personal sorrows, all of which I shared with my viewers because of the nature of our show.

Shirley, Norma and their children, Ann and Tony, at their home in 1971.

and received his medical degree from Yale Medical School. After serving at Children's Hospital in Boston as a pediatric cardiologist for sixteen years, he is now head of the Cardio Vascular Intensive Care Unit at Lucile Packard Children's Hospital at Stanford University in Palo Alto, California. He is married to Andrea Fish and they have two daughters, Amalia and Julianna. His father, Joel Roth, a retired judge, lives in Great Falls. Steve and his family visit as often as they can.

In 1971, after Steve had returned to live with his grandparents and to be near his father in Washington, we learned we couldn't have our own children, so we decided to adopt an older child as we had been exposed to the lives of older children through Steve. We contacted the Lutheran Social Services. They were a part of Arena, a world-wide adoption agency, and at Easter time they called us not about one child but two, a brother and sister from Canada who were available for adoption. They sent us a picture and it was love at first sight. The little girl was nine, with short brown hair and blue eyes and a big smile. Our favorite name for a daughter was Ann, after my late sister. Not only was her first name Ann, but her middle name was Norma. Her seven–year–old brother, Tony, had dark brown hair and eyes and a sweet smile on his shy face.

They came to our home for the long Easter weekend and we knew we were meant to be together. They came to live with us for good that summer and we became a family when the adoption ceremony took place on July 12, 1972.

Our children are now grown. Our daughter, Ann Longfellow, works in the restaurant business as a cook and Tony Ashby is a driver for a delivery service. They have given us much happiness and three grandsons. Ann has two sons: Bill Schrader, who has graduated from Great Falls High School and is following in Ann's footsteps to be a cook and Jack Schrader, who is in the eighth grade and is interested in art and music. Tony has one son, Dusty Ashby, a sophomore at Great Falls High School who loves sports, especially football and basketball.

On July 12, 1992, the twentieth anniversary of their adoption, Ann wrote this to us:

> *To Our Parents,*
> *Mom and Dad, I speak for both Tony and myself. Twenty years ago you gave us a home, a name and love. We grew and shared as most families do. We even had our hard times. But we had good times too.*
> *So today we say Thank you for everything you have done for us.*
> *As more years pass, I hope we can keep growing and loving each other as families do. Mom, Dad, We Love You!*

In 1981, my mother, Ella Mehmke, died of cancer at the age of seventy-six—a great loss for me. Mom loved people and was an eternal optimist. I credit her with my love of people and my optimism and am grateful to have been her daughter. She was a great supporter of everything I did and a favorite travel companion. Shirley said he had done enough traveling when he was in the service, so he sent me off, with his blessing, on trips with my mother. She loved to travel, as I did, and she accompanied me to a number of American Women in Radio and Television National Conventions, and enjoyed every one of them.

Family, friends and viewers were there once again to help me through this difficult time in my life. Here is my favorite saying about friendship: Friendship divides our grief and multiplies our happiness.

So he called me up one night and said, "Norma, would you like to get married?" "Yes," I said. "Who is this?"

LIVE *Television*

The unique thing about a show like *Today in Montana* was that viewers felt like they had a stake in the program. They supplied the jokes, the poems, the thoughts, the ideas for guests, and best of all, thousands of them got to appear with me on the air. We got to know each other on and off the air. I made many speeches throughout the state, such as at a commencement in Rudyard, at the Seed Show in Harlem and at Woman's Week in Bozeman and judged beauty pageants such as the Montana Territorial Centennial Queen Contest in Great Falls. I welcomed each opportunity to meet more of our viewers and to get ideas for future guests. That's why to this day people still stop me and reminisce about when they were a guest on the show, comment about a program we did ten, twenty, thirty or even forty years ago, or heard me speak in their hometown.

We kept our audience informed every weekday morning with news and weather, and brought into their homes visits with fellow Montanans as well as celebrities and people from throughout the nation and the world, covering nearly every field of endeavor from entertainment to politics.

Because our cast of *Today in Montana* enjoyed being on the air together, our audience claimed us as part of their family.

You might say I grew up with my audience, starting my career as a young single woman in my twenties, gaining more experience in broadcasting with each passing year, becoming a wife, a mother, and finally a grandmother. I also brought to our audience reports on the many trips I took and the fascinating people I was privileged to meet from Princess Margaret to First Lady Pat Nixon.

I believe two things were responsible for the success of *Today in Montana*: The first was the longevity of the *Today in Montana* show. The second was the extended time I was on the air with the same show, which is something unique in a medium where shows and personalities come and go so quickly.

It was a wonderful ride and I was happy to share it for so long with our loyal audience.

—2—
On Camera: Celebrities

To host and produce a live television show in the 1960s, '70s and '80s was a glorious experience because of all the famous people who came through Montana: people ranging from entertainer Bob Hope to First Lady Pat Nixon, from minister and author Dr. Norman Vincent Peale to actor Clint Eastwood. Also, in the course of my travels to conventions, I met and interviewed famous people outside of Montana as well.

Many of my guests on *Today in Montana* were headliners for the Montana State Fair, which is held each summer in Great Falls. Others were sponsored by the Great Falls Junior League for their celebrity series from 1968 to 1985. Others were honored guests of the annual C.M. Russell Auction. I was very lucky to be at the right place at the right time to meet and interview many of these people, and the celebrities themselves seemed to welcome the television exposure. Certainly the groups who sponsored them welcomed the publicity for their events. And, during that time, talent fees and speaking fees seemed to be more reasonable than they are today.

After 1985, the popular Junior League Celebrity Series was discontinued because its venue, the Fox Theater in the Holiday Village, was to be torn down to make room for more parking. Also, at that time, women were going back to work, which had an impact on ticket sales for these weekday morning lectures.

Over the years, I talked to celebrities from all corners of the entertainment world. I spoke with singers Eddy Arnold, Johnny Cash, Jimmy Dean, Dale Evans, Tennessee Ernie Ford, Marilyn McCoo, Marie Osmond, the Osmond Brothers, Roberta Peters, Robert Merrill, Ronnie Milsap, Ann Murray, Jim Nabors and Roy Rogers. I interviewed movie stars including Rex Allen, Noah "Pidg" Beery Jr., Peter Fonda, Lillian Gish, Celeste Holm, George

---

I admit I had a crush on him. Called the most exciting new entertainer in show-business and a very good-looking man to boot, he had a devastating effect on the ladies, including me. At the end of our visit, he leaned over and kissed me. The recorder captured the sound of the kiss!

Montgomery and Dale Robertson. I spoke with television stars, including Angie Dickinson, John McIntire, Carroll O'Connor, Denver Pyle and Marlo Thomas. Comedians Red Skelton and George Gobel appeared on the show. I also interviewed Olympic gold-medal gymnast Mary Lou Retton.

Over the years, I also featured national broadcasters, including Tom Brokaw, Walter Cronkite, Sam Donaldson, Nancy Dickerson, Hugh Downs, Pauline Frederick, Paul Harvey, Charles Kuralt, Charles Osgood, Jane Pauley, Leslie Stahl and Barbara Walters.

Tennessee Ernie Ford, the headliner for the 1967 Montana State Fair, on the set with Norma.

Celebrity In-Depth Interviews: Senator Margaret Chase Smith

In April 1964, when I was in Washington, D.C., with the Montana delegation promoting the Montana Territorial Centennial, I was able to arrange an interview with Republican Senator Margaret Chase Smith of Maine. Montana First Lady Betty Babcock accompanied me and we interviewed Margaret in her office in the Senate office building. I brought my recorder along and my camera to tape the interview and take pictures of her for *Today in Montana*. We were impressed with the Senator's warmth, soft New England accent, and her snow-white hair.

At that time, Smith was the first and only woman who had been elected to serve in both the House and Senate of the United States. She was also the first woman to seek the nomination for president of the United States. She ran in the national primaries in 1964.

After she asked us to make ourselves comfortable, I asked Margaret what most inspired her to seek the nomination for president.

She looked at me, and replied, "I would have to answer that it was my mail. I received mail for a year or more from every state in the Union asking if I wouldn't give serious consideration to being a candidate for the presidency."

I asked her what her reaction was to the recent Illinois primary in which she had a very good showing.

44

She grinned and answered:

> I'm delighted. I have been saying all along if I could translate the warmth and hospitality that was extended to me in Illinois in votes I would be very happy. The last I counted we had over 206,000 votes. I only spent about eighty-five dollars, which makes them pretty cheap. There is a small group of very brilliant and very fine young men and some very dedicated women who took hold of this candidacy of mine and I think they deserve the credit for it.

I asked her if she had an organization that was helping her seek the nomination.

> I don't have an organization and the reason is because the minute you start having an organization, it costs money. You may remember when I announced I said that I didn't have any organization. Could a candidate whose only asset was twenty-four years of public service get recognition? I have had to avoid any signs of or spending money.

I asked her to comment on how her constituents and Senate colleagues reacted to her drive for the presidential nomination.

> There have been some very interesting reactions. For instance, Senator George Aiken of Vermont was one of those who urged me to do this. He has been a very loyal supporter even after the New Hampshire primary. He had not lost confidence in me, so you can imagine what this Illinois vote has done for him. But generally speaking, the Senators have been very kind, very gracious in their attitude toward my candidacy, though I presume they have their own preferences.

Would she consider, I asked, accepting the second place spot on the Republican ticket—as vice president of the United States?

> As long as I am a candidate for president, I would not consider any other position. I have one of the finest positions

Network broadcaster Jane Pauley and Norma on the set of NBC's *Today* show in New York City.

in the country in the United States Senate. I have increased my majorities each time that I have been a candidate and that's why I am a candidate for president. Let's leave it there.

I asked her what kind of reaction she got when she was out shaking hands—say in Chicago—from male voters. She noted, to my surprise, that in her years in politics she had not really seen a difference between the support she had received from male and female voters, despite her close scrutiny.

Are you generally well accepted? I asked. Or do they harass you and wonder if you are really serious about this?

No, surprising as it may be, and this is I think surprising to everyone, men usually talk to me about my record and my integrity and about the job that I have done through the years. The women usually talk to me about the courage I had to go into the race. In 1948, when I first ran for United States Senator, the issue used against me was the Senate was no place for a woman. Yet my primary papers were signed by sixty men and forty women.

What do you think you have done, I asked, to win the support and confidence of your male colleagues in the Senate?

I have been here a long time. I was in the House a long time before I came over to the Senate. I worked with their wives, worked with their staffs, because I was a secretary at the first of my time there. I have worked with them in committees. If I were to point out any one thing, I would say that I have always accepted my responsibility as a Senator and never asked for any special privileges, and I assure you, I never got any. I have heard my colleagues say of me, 'She always does her homework. When she comes into a meeting, she knows what she wants to do and she does it.' That is a very great compliment here.

I noticed that she was wearing a red rose in her lapel—which was her signature accessory—and I asked her when she started wearing a red rose.

She laughed and touched the red rose that she was wearing. "I started that in the early days when I first came to Washington, even

> **CHARLEY PRIDE**
> I interviewed country western singer Charley Pride, who got his start singing in clubs in East Helena and Great Falls when he was a minor league baseball player in Montana. He was in town in 1983 and in 1988 with his wife Rozene. They were honored guests for the annual C. M. Russell Auction. I interviewed him in March 1988 on his birthday. When I asked him how old he was, he replied, "Plenty nine."

before I was in Congress, largely because someone gave me a little lapel vase and I wanted to make use of it," she said. "It grew to be such a habit. I wear pretty much the same kind of clothes every day and a bright red rose, or a bright yellow rose, sort of perks me up."

I then asked Smith to describe her working day—as I had heard she had one of the most rigorous work schedules in Congress.

> It is a long one. I try to get into the office before 8 a.m., sometimes earlier. I like to look the mail over and read the headlines from my own state newspapers that are always a day late. I can do that best before I start to committee. I have a very heavy committee load. I am in one to four or five committees beginning at 10 a.m. I am fourth-ranking Republican on the twenty-seven member Appropriations Committee. I am second- ranking Republican on the Armed Services Committee and the top-ranking Republican on the Space Committee. I don't stay in the Senate chambers as much as some people do because I do my committee work and I have a great deal of mail.

Senator Smith had one of the finest records of any senator for being present at roll call votes. She said the last roll call she had missed was on June 1, 1955. She laughs. "I was told by the then- Majority Leader, Lyndon Johnson, that there wouldn't be any votes that afternoon and I went to New York to receive an honorary degree from Columbia University," she said. "I got back at 6 p.m. that night and got in just after the second roll call vote."

I asked her why she felt that being present for these roll call votes was so important—when other senators often took off to their home states and frequently missed them.

> When I first started on this job, I had two objectives. One was to stay on the job to which I was elected. Two was to stay close to the people who I represent. People voted and elected me to attend to my duties in the Senate. So I

VINCENT PRICE

Vincent Price, the actor, best known for his roles as villains in such movies as *House of Wax* and *The Pit and the Pendulum*, was a celebrity series speaker in 1973. When I asked him how he had kept looking so youthful and dynamic, he said, "Nobody looks older really. You can meet a ninety-year-old who is as vital and young as a person who is fifty or younger. I do a lot of things and I like to work and I'm very pleased with my life. I feel that's the one thing that keeps you active and interested and young."

have not missed many votes in my 6,000 or 8,000 votes through the years.

I haven't missed getting back to the State of Maine at least once a month now for over seven years. And following the fall adjournment, I go to Maine and before I do anything else, I cover the state. I use eight weeks and I speak to all kinds of groups. I listen to their questions and in doing that I am better able to know what they are thinking and what they are wanting. Then every sixth year when election time comes, I don't have to start campaigning as strenuously as other people do. I've done it all the years before.

I concluded the interview by asking Senator Smith about the surprising song about her that was presented at the National Women's Press Club in Washington just the evening before our interview.

It was an annual dinner for the Editors Association, and individual members sang

PHOTO BY "DOC" KAMINSKI, 1963

ROBERT GOULET

Robert Goulet, actor and night club singer, whom I had seen play the role of Lancelot in *Camelot* on Broadway in New York, remains one of the most heart-stopping guests I have interviewed. The interview took place in 1963 at the Ambassador Hotel in Los Angeles where I was attending the Advertising Association of the West Convention as a delegate from the Great Falls Advertising Club.

I learned in advance that Robert was the headliner at the Coconut Grove in the Ambassador Hotel and I arranged to interview him when I was there. Armed with my reel-to-reel tape recorder, I recorded the interview on audiotape.

It was very disconcerting for me, a young woman in her twenties, to be looking nearly nose to nose with Robert Goulet with only a tape recorder between us. Robert was six feet tall, dark, handsome, and his baritone voice was magnificent. I admit I had a crush on him. Called the most exciting new entertainer in show business and a very good-looking man to boot, he had a devastating effect on the ladies, including me. At the end of our visit, he leaned over and kissed me. The recorder captured the sound of the kiss! I never saw him in person again, but I'll never forget the moment.

songs for each candidate beginning with President Lyndon Johnson, who was a candidate for re-election.

It looked as though I was going to be left out. There was no card for me. But at the very end, the whole group of girls who had been singing came on to the platform with the music and sang this very, very, very good song to me, which in so many words was saying I was their candidate. It brought great applause from around the room and it was one of the highest tributes I shall probably ever get. It was called, "Hello, Maggie," and it was sung to the tune of "Hello, Dolly."

I asked her what advice she would give other women who might want to enter politics. Or what advice she would give to women who might look to her as a guide.

In a speech that I have often given to young women, 'The Challenge to Women,' I try very hard to help young women realize that home is basic. Perhaps the most lasting and basic influence of women is in the home—for behind all men, great or small, are women. And the fight for decent conditions in communities, for improvement in food, housing, school, health, and recreational facilities must be led by the women of the home—the wives and the mothers.

We all want to be married and have a home. We all want to have families. But that is all the more reason we should be active in civic affairs, and that is why we should be willing to serve on education boards, hospital boards, church groups—to make the community in which we live the very best there is. And after those children are grown, gone to college or married, those same women who have become very experienced can do a great deal of public service and I hope they do that.

I do caution them, however, that if they don't like people, if they don't enjoy people, it is going to be very difficult for them to be in politics. If they will develop their personality, be themselves, don't try to copy someone else, stay a lady, accept their responsibilities, they can do much more than I have done because their chances are much greater than mine were when I was their age.

Whether or not there is a future in politics for women

"In a speech that I have often given to young women, 'The Challenge to Women,' I try very hard to help young women realize that home is basic. Perhaps the most lasting and basic influence of women is in the home—for behind all men, great or small, are women."

> "The home then should not be severed from the government. In fact, there has been too little of the home and too much government in the home. The most obvious and natural way to reverse this trend is to put more of home governors in the government—and this means women."

depends upon the women themselves. If they have the sufficient desire and determination to hold not only public office but to organize politically and vote in blocks and elect qualified women candidates, then there is most definitely a future in politics for women. The inescapable fact is that they hold the control of the public offices with their majority voting power.

Will they exercise that power? I think that they will if they are made to realize that they hold the power. Organized women's power has been forcefully proved if the incentive is there.

Basically, the incentive and the attraction of more women in higher public office should stem from the fundamental fact that women are the governors of the home. They make the rules of the home; they execute and enforce the rules of the home; and they interpret the rules of the home. And the home is the most fundamental form of government. Our community governments are no more than a federation of individual home governments.

The home then should not be severed from the government. In fact, there has been too little of the home and too much government in the home. The most obvious and natural way to reverse this trend is to put more of home governors in the government—and this means women.

It is ironic to me that no woman since Senator Smith has run for the nomination for president of the United States in either party. Senator Smith died in 1995 at the age of ninety-eight. Her papers are in the Margaret Chase Smith Library in Skowhegan, Maine.

Elizabeth "Liz" Carpenter, Press Secretary for Lady Bird Johnson

Another interview I did in the spring of 1964 in Washington, D. C. was with Elizabeth "Liz" Carpenter, press secretary and staff director for First Lady Claudia Alta or "Lady Bird" Johnson for *Today in Montana*. This interview was run in its entirety on NBC Radio's nationwide program *Monitor* in 1964 and excerpts were used on *Today in Montana*.

This was my first visit to the White House and when I stepped inside the most visited house in America, I had to pinch myself to

LAWRENCE WELK SHOW PERFORMERS

In 1966, Lawrence Welk brought acts from his popular television show to the state fair, and I was able to interview pianist Joanne Castle, the vocal trio of the Lennon Sisters and the dance team of Bobby Burgess and Barbara Boylan on *Today in Montana*. These talented performers were friendly, fun-loving and easy to talk to. They stayed after our program to have their pictures taken with the crew. I took Bobby and Barbara Boylan to meet my mother and stepfather at their farm east of town and we kept in touch after they left. I attended Barbara's wedding in California and I still exchange Christmas cards with Bobby and his family. He married Kristie Floren, the daughter of Myron Floren, accordionist on the Lawrence Welk show and they have four grown children.

Here is a letter from Bobby sent on May 30, 1968, from his home in Studio City, California.

The Lennon Sisters, from left: Kathy, Janet and Peggy

Dear Norma,
I got my mail so late at the studio I guess I missed your visit out here to Sunny Calif. Sure sorry! I'd have liked to have seen you again, or at least talked to you on the phone.

You sound as though you like your work as much as I do. I'm also in my seventh season on the Welk Show and was told today I may be put on the production staff next year.

Oh, guess you'd like to know about Barbara. She's expecting her first in Dec.

We did a show together last week and after I'd gotten through tossing her around, she breathlessly told me she was two months along.

Well Norma, I still say Great Falls people are about the friendliest I've met anywhere on my tours.

I hope to see you soon.
Best Wishes to you -
Your Dancin' Friend,
Bobby Burgess

P.S. Just bought a four-unit apartment house and am living in it here in Studio City. Say hi to everyone.

Bobby sent me a postcard in August of 1966 after he and Barbara had attended the wedding and reception of Luci Johnson to Pat Nugent in Washington, D. C. He wrote:

Norma, Bobby Burgess and Barbara Boylan

You'll never guess what was the hit dance of the evening? The polka! Of course that's one of our favorites and we had a ball. They also played watusis, and Luci and Pat and all joined in. We enjoyed changing partners with them and meeting President Johnson and Lady Bird. The buffet was delicious and we had the time of our lives. We still say Great Falls is our favorite town as far as friendly people.

believe I was there. I used my trusty recorder to tape the interview with Liz in her East Wing office. A short, stocky woman with a Southern accent, she beamed from ear to ear when we met and her friendly manner made me feel immediately at home. An experienced journalist, she was well-prepared for my questions.

I began by asking her how she got her job. She answered with practiced aplomb.

I began working for the vice president shortly after he was nominated in Los Angeles in 1960. I happened to be covering, as a reporter, the Republican convention in Chicago. The phone rang and I heard him say, "I am nominated for vice president. Lady Bird is going to need some help. Can you take a leave of absence to share the great adventure of our lives?" I said, "Give me twenty-four hours to think about it, and I decided I would take up flying, though I'd been opposed to it before."

Noting her Southern accent, I asked her where she was from.

I am from Texas. I grew up in the President's home district. As you probably know, his career has really been straight up the political ladder. He was a secretary to a congressman, which is a very good way to learn how to be a congressman. Then he was a congressman for twelve years, a senator for twelve years, vice president for three, and he is now presi-

BOB HOPE

Bob Hope came to Great Falls as a headliner for the state fair in August 1970. During his media interviews in the Rainbow Hotel's ballroom, he lived up to his reputation of being down-to-earth, funny and accessible to everyone. When I asked him if he had ever considered running for political office, he said, "I don't think I'd like it. I like what I do now. I'm not qualified to be in politics. Ronald Reagan thinks Sacramento is a stepping stone. If he ever becomes president we won't have stamps, we'll have 8x10" glossies."

dent. I think if you checked your history on presidents, you would find that he has more accumulated service in the government arm than any other man who has served in that office.

I asked her how many women she had on her staff to assist with all the things that came in for Mrs. Johnson.

Not enough. We have three or four girls who help do a great many tasks. It is amazing how much variety there is. A lot of it is answering the phone calls of newspaper people every day. We have about 150 phone calls that come in here every single day, wanting to know everything, from why Luci changed the spelling of her name, to an advance text on Mrs. Johnson's speech at the Eleanor Roosevelt Memorial Fund. If you are trying to do a conscientious job, you try to give a satisfactory answer in the best and shortest time.

As this house belongs to all the people of the country, the general public feels that they have a claim on the First Family, whoever it may be. There are about 1,000 letters a week—apart from the tremendous mail that the president receives—that come in to the east side of the White House, which is the family side.

The letters revolve around three subjects generally: women, dogs and old brocades. About twenty of these 1,000 letters go to the two teenage daughters. I'm told by the lady who has handled the correspondence section of the White House for about twenty years that when the Kennedy children lived here, much of the mail was in block printing from children. Most of our mail to the Johnson teenagers are from teenagers who identify with them. It has made me very proud of teenagers, to read those letters. I think they often get a black eye and you would be surprised what thoughtful citizens they are if you saw the letters.

Then there is always curiosity about the pets in the White House. We have three dogs now and one of the questions I got at a press conference was, "Are the dogs happy?" I replied, "Yes." They said, "Where do they live?" I said, "They live in the White House dog house." They said, "How do you

Johnny Cash with Norma in Great Falls in 1976.

JOAN CRAWFORD

Joan Crawford, a movie star who won an Oscar in 1945 for *Mildred Pierce*, was available for interviews during the 1968 American Women in Radio and Television Western Area Conference in Los Angeles that I was attending as a Montana delegate. Since she was my mother's favorite actress, I looked forward to meeting her.

Joan was serving on the board of Pepsi Cola, a role she stepped into following the death of her husband, who had been chairman of the company. Two bottles of Pepsi sat on the table as we did our interview. She was elegantly dressed in a pink and aqua floral dress and a matching turban.

I asked her what it was like to work with Bette Davis in the 1962 movie, *Whatever Happened to Baby Jane?*

"It was great," she replied, as she flicked an ash from her cigarette into the ashtray. "As a matter of fact I put the deal together. It was good box office chemistry."

When I asked her how she felt when she won an Academy Award for her role in *Mildred Pierce*, she laughed and said, "Terrible. I was at home in bed with a 104-degree temperature."

When I told her that she was my mother, Ella Mehmke's, favorite actress, she gave me an autographed picture. It said, "To Ella, Love, Joan Crawford." My mother framed it and had it in a prominent place in her home.

After interviewing Joan in May 1968, we exchanged three letters. This was a letter she wrote after I sent her the picture of the two of us. The letter was sent from her home in New York and the cancellation had the Pepsi slogan: "Taste that beats the others cold."

The letter dated May 31, 1968, reads:

My Dear Norma,

Thank you very much for your sweet letter and for the lovely color picture of you and me. How dear you were to have a print made for me. Your face is so happy and lovely and charming!

I am delighted that you are pleased with the interview we had. I hope you'll have some nice mail and comments about it.

Bless you—and thank you for writing. I hope we'll see each other again very soon.

Joan

know they are happy?" I said, "Because I'm in there most of the time."

Then there are a lot of people who are interested in the furniture of the White House. There is history connected with almost every settee and painting, and there are old brocade and drapery buffs. They don't like to have you move a chair more than one inch. If you do that, they are likely to protest. Some of them will come up with suggestions on how to redecorate the house.

I asked her if she attempted to answer all of the mail that came in.

Yes, we certainly do! Mrs. Johnson is very conscientious about that and she likes to see that the writers are supplied with good answers. There is a curator here who is full of knowledge and information, not only about the furnishings themselves, but also about the people who occupy this house.

I have been educating myself. I have learned, for example, the place where the swimming pool is in the White House. It was built for Franklin Roosevelt because as you know he had polio and this was the therapy he could enjoy when he was confined in the White House. The swimming pool is in the place where Thomas Jefferson once had his chicken house. The library of the White House, which is on the ground floor, was once an open [area] where Abigail Adams kept her cows. I was telling this one time at a press briefing and someone spoke up and said "that means we have moved from moos to news."

I asked her to describe how much Mrs. Johnson had to travel and what kinds of trips she took.

She has tried to have at least one trip outside of Washington each month, which gives her an opportunity to see an interesting project where the community has worked with the federal government or sometimes where the community has just done it itself, to make life a little bit better for the citizens of that town.

She feels this is valuable because she can be an extra set of eyes and ears for the president, who is pretty much confined to his desk, and also it widens her own horizons.

"As this house belongs to all the people of the country, the general public feels that they have a claim on the First Family, whoever it may be."

Then I think anyone who goes along on these trips as a number of the press do, would tell you that it is very nice for the people to have their efforts saluted when sometimes they are overlooked.

I referred to the unpredictability of the Johnson family and asked Liz how it affected her work.

> It gives me lots of challenges that I try to live up to and I think it builds character. Sometimes you may tear your hair, but I would want them to always be spontaneous people. I think that's one of their charms. I think the President, particularly, is a very warm person. He sees people standing outside the fence of the White House and wants to go out and shake hands with them. I think he ought to be able to do this without sending an engraved invitation to the press room to come along with him. Sometimes they seem to expect this. Also tornadoes, earthquakes and schedules do not run on time for briefings.

I had heard that Lady Bird Johnson was much lovelier in person than in many of her photographs, so I asked Liz, if this was true, all the while blushing at the directness of my question.

> She has a lot of expression in her manner. With expressive people, their beauty comes through only when they are at ease or when you capture them at a time they least expect it. She has had some very nice pictures taken, but so often when people who go through a receiving line say to her, "You are so much prettier than your pictures." Her reply, which is always in good humor is, "I'm going to have to make good friends with the photographers."

I asked her about Mrs. Johnson's hobbies.

> Hobbies are something that Mrs. Johnson hasn't thought about in a long time. She has a project that she is very interested in and which I think will mean a great deal later on if we can persuade her to let it be published. Ever since November 22, 1963 [Johnson became president the day of John F. Kennedy's assassination], she speaks into her little 'talking machine,' as she calls it, to describe the

---

"We have three dogs now and one of the questions I got at a press conference was, 'Are the dogs happy?' I replied, 'Yes.' They said, 'Where do they live?' I said, 'They live in the White House dog house.'"

events that have occurred, the people who have come to this house, and some of the conversations that took place. I don't know any First Lady who has ever done such a record. I think it will be invaluable because Mrs. Johnson majored in journalism and has a gift of words. I think if she had had time in her life, she could have written very lovely essays, probably poetry, because she has good word discipline. I hope that some day this will be a part of history.

(Mrs. Johnson's *White House Diary* was published in 1970.)

During the interview, I asked Liz which recipe Lady Bird Johnson supplied for the *First Ladies Cookbook* that Montana's First Lady Betty Babcock put together and published in 1964.

Elizabeth laughed and answered.

It is Deer Meat Sausage. You take half a deer and half a hog, and mix them with lots of salt and pepper. We think of Montana as a state very akin to Texas in its taste for good and hearty living and food.

I thanked Liz for the interview and presented her with a Montana Big Sky souvenir book for the First Lady and invited her and the Johnsons to come to Montana for the 1964 Centennial Celebration.

Abigail Van Buren

In 1987, Abigail Van Buren, who was known for her widely syndicated newspaper advice column, *Dear Abby*, came to Great Falls for the Montana Deaconess Medical Center's Senior Care Symposium. I introduced her at the symposium and interviewed her for *Today in Montana*.

When I met her, Abby was approaching her seventieth birthday. Born on the fourth of July, 1918, she had been writing for newspapers since 1956. Her twin sister, Ann Landers, was also an advice columnist. Abby was barely five feet tall, with dark, perfectly coiffed hair, large sparkling eyes and a beautiful smile. It was obvious she felt right at home with the public and enjoyed giving speeches. She was a huge hit with the Symposium audience that

PATRICIA NEAL

Patricia Neal, who won an Oscar in 1963 for her role in *Hud*, came to Great Falls in 1982 as a speaker for the Junior League Celebrity Series. She wore a tiny replica of her Oscar on a chain around her neck. I had read of her great love for Gary Cooper, the Montana actor with whom she had starred in *The Fountainhead* in 1949, and I asked her if she would comment on him. She sighed and said, "I just adored him. He was the love of my life. He was a heavenly man."

packed the Civic Center. The organizers had to supply a box for her to stand on at the podium, because she was so tiny.

In our interview, I asked her to describe her philosophy about aging.

> I think everything should be done by men as well as women—whether it's plastic surgery, calisthenics or meditation—to keep you young and healthy and useful. Look as good as you can for your years. Don't lie about it. I think the trick is to keep doing something. If you are interested in something it keeps you interesting.

Abby said she loved writing her column. She received eight to ten thousand letters a week and had seven women on her staff to help process the mail. Many people did not sign their letters, but those who did she would refer to agencies that could help them in their area. She maintained files of agencies in each city that carried her column. She said sometimes if people were desperate and included their phone number she would call them.

I was struck by her kindness, her compassion and her concern for others. With her quick wit, yet her caring and common sense approach to her reader's questions, I could see why her column had been so popular for so long. I asked her what was the most asked about subject.

"Relationships," she replied without hesitation. "All kinds of relationships—husband and wife, parent and child, worker and boss. You name it. If people could figure out how to live in harmony with one another, this would be a much better world."

When I asked her how she had come up with the pen name, Abby—whose real name is Pauline Friedman Phillips—she said she started with the Old Testament.

> I looked in the book of I Samuel and I found Abigail. "David said to her, 'Blessed be thy advice.' For my last

Advice columnist Abigail Van Buren of Dear Abby who spoke in Great Falls in 1987.

name, I chose the last name of our eighth president Martin Van Buren. I liked the sound of it. I thought Abigail Van Buren would be a super name for an advice columnist.

Abby served with actress Elizabeth Taylor on the board of the American Foundation for AIDS Research. She had this advice for anyone who is sexually active.

> Be very careful with the people who you get close to. If you have any reason at all to believe that you are carrying AIDS, get tested. If you have ever had a blood transfusion, get tested. The only possible cure can be found in research.

When I asked her about drug and alcohol use in today's young people she said she felt it was our country's number one problem. She looked very serious as she talked. "Peer pressure is what tempts these kids, she said quietly."

> We need to educate our young people at a very early age about the dangers of drugs and alcohol. They are very addictive. I would tell any young person not to use drugs and alcohol—and I would tell them not to spend time with people who do.

On a personal note, after the interview Abby admired my false eyelashes. She had previously worn them but they wouldn't stay on and she complained that she could not get the glue to stick. When I assured her the glue I used was guaranteed to work, she decided to try them again. We got in my car and drove to Merle Norman Cosmetics Studio in downtown Great Falls and she bought herself a pair. Owner Carole Henderson was thrilled to have such a famous customer.

Abigail Van Buren wrote her column until she retired in 2002, the same year her twin sister Ann Landers died. The popular *Dear Abby* column continues and is written by Abby's daughter, Jeanne Phillips.

Chet Huntley

In 1968, I interviewed NBC Newscaster and Montana native Chet Huntley in our KRTV studios about his book, *The Generous Years*, which had just been published. Chet was touring the state, promoting his book, when I caught up with him. A tall man, with rugged good looks, a hearty laugh and one of the best voices in

---

...After the interview Abby admired my false eyelashes. She had previously worn them but they wouldn't stay on and she complained that she could not get the glue to stick. When I assured her the glue I used was guaranteed to work, she decided to try them again.

broadcasting, Chet talked about his book that described his experiences growing up in Montana between 1913 and 1927.

Born in Cardwell, Montana, Chet grew up in towns along the Northern Pacific line, including Bozeman, Big Timber, Logan, Reedpoint, Saco, Scobey, Whitehall and Willow Creek because his father was a railroad telegrapher. He won a scholarship to Montana State University in 1929. Three years of premed led nowhere, until he won a national oratory contest and scholarship to Seattle's Cornish School of Arts in 1932. A year later, he switched to the University of Washington. In 1934, he got his first job in broadcasting, when he was hired by Seattle's KCBC radio. He worked on the West Coast until 1956, when he was hired by NBC in New York to cover, with David Brinkley, the Democratic national convention in Chicago and the Republican national convention in San Francisco. The *Huntley-Brinkley Report* began October 29, 1956, and aired for fifteen years.

NBC Newscaster and Montana native Chet Huntley, who received a Montana Territorial Centennial medallion from Norma at his New York office in 1963.

It was a special treat to welcome Chet to *Today in Montana*. I had met him four years before, when I lived in New York. We were both at a Montana Club of New York party at the Gramercy Park Hotel penthouse. The club was for displaced Montanans living in New York and was organized with the help of alumni offices in the University of Montana in Missoula and Montana State University in Bozeman. It wasn't long before our club had 700 members. We had people from all walks of life including entertainers, executives, lawyers and secretaries. Chet, who was always cordial to everyone, was our most famous member.

In 1964, Chet narrated a film I had written about my hometown of Helena, *Last Chance Gulch*. When I called him, I said, "I can't offer you any money, but I can offer you fame." He laughed and said, "Send me the script." In a short time, he returned the taped narration, adding several of his own words, including these: "ubiquitous" to describe dancing girls and "sky pilot" to describe the ax-wielding minister who had chopped down the hangman's tree in Helena. His magnificent voice added a great deal of professionalism to the film. I was deeply grateful to him.

The next time I saw Chet was in April 1964 in Washington, D.C. He was master of ceremonies for the Montana Centennial Train Dinner where Senator Mike Mansfield spoke and President Lyndon Johnson made a surprise appearance.

At that dinner, Chet thrilled the audience by reading his Montana statement, which I later repeated on *Today in Montana* and made copies available to my viewers:

> Have you ever stood on the platform of the depot in Whitehall and watched the North Coast Limited snake down the eastern abutment of the Continental Divide into Pipestone and on into the Whitehall block with Pete Ross, Ramblin' Jack Wolverton or Jim Berry at the throttle?
>
> Have you ever heard the lonely wail of the Empire Builder send the echoes flying across the wintry Saco flats, the Milk River, and up on the North Bench to Whitewater and the Canadian Line?
>
> Do you remember the angry and excruciating snorts...the blasts of mechanical vituperation...as the great articulated malleys pulled a hundred cars and a caboose over Bridger Pass into the fertile Gallatin Valley?

OLIVIA DeHAVILLAND

Olivia DeHavilland, the only surviving cast member of the epic film *Gone With the Wind*, came to Great Falls as a part of the 1973 Junior League Celebrity Series. A beautiful, elegant, soft-spoken woman, she commented on her role as Melanie, which won her an Academy Award nomination for best supporting actress. She said, "She was a perfectly loving person. It was love that directed her in her relationships and all of her relationships were happy and successful."

In 1964, Chet narrated a film I had written about my hometown of Helena, <u>Last Chance Gulch</u>. When I called him, I said, "I can't offer you any money, but I can offer you fame." He laughed and said, "Send me the script."

Have you ever sung the music of Montana names: Choteau, Cascade, Missoula, Pend O'Reille, Big Horn, Carbon, Sweetgrass, Stillwater, Silver Bow, and Glacier? Roundup, Little Butte, Judith Gap, Harlowtown, Armington, Spion Kop, Great Falls? And the ridiculous little name of Two Dot?

The Lodge Pole Meadows, Half-Moon Park, Rattlesnake Canyon, Last Chance Gulch, Meaderville, and Stinky Creek? The Belts and Little Belts, Bitterroots and Tobacco Roots, Big Horns and Absarokees, the Crazies and the Little Rockies.

Do you know Deer Lodge, Red Lodge, or Lodge Grass, Plentywood, Scobey, Cut Bank, Boulder, Ekalaka, Glendive, Kalispell, Big Timber and Neihart? And what about the Madison, the Gallatin, the Jefferson, the Milk, the Yellowstone, the Powder, the Bitterroot, and the Flathead, and the great Missouri, without which the Mississippi would be only a gentle Thames or Tiber?

Have you ever seen dawn at the Gates of the Mountains or listened to the morning call of a meadowlark in a Lewistown wheat field? Have you seen the day's new sun strike great explosions of light from the craggy facets of the Spanish Peaks?

Have you seen the Crazies by moonlight or have you gathered stardust from Hebgen or Flathead? Have you seen Old Hollowtop silhouetted against the setting sun, standing immutably as a sentinel over the dusk-filled Gallatin Valley?

These are some of the experiences and places and names that bind us together, for we know them intimately and we can feel that they are ours.

A few days later, Chet and his wife Tippy, were master and mistress of ceremonies at the Montana Centennial Train Dinner at the Commodore Hotel in New York City. I organized the dinner from Montana and was thrilled when they accepted the job. One of the highlights was a performance by Montie Montana Jr. doing trick roping atop his horse. I had to arrange for a service elevator and I had to hire carpenters to build a ramp so Montie and his horse could get to the stage.

The last time I saw Chet was in February 1970, at a press conference in the Governor's Reception room in the State Capitol in

Helena, when he and Tippy announced plans for Big Sky, a $19 million dollar resort, situated forty-five miles south of Bozeman, near Yellowstone Park in southwestern Montana. The resort was to be backed by Chrysler Realty Corporation. Chet retired from his job as co-anchor on the NBC *Nightly News* on August 1, 1970, wrapping up a thirty-six year broadcasting career. He was excited about his new venture.

Chet said Big Sky had been a dream of his for twenty years. In our interview, his voice was clear and sure as he talked about his philosophy behind the resort:

> I have long thought that there must be a way to bring hundreds of thousands of our fellow Americans and foreign visitors to Montana and let them see this scenery and get them acquainted with Montana's special breed of people...so that they can enjoy the climate out here and the environment. I want visitors to appreciate it and admire it without damaging it, without exploiting the land, without mining it and ruining it.
>
> Technology has helped us in this undertaking. There are now ways to do this so that you can provide for visitors and give them every degree of comfort and even luxury they desire and still not hurt the land or clutter up the environment or ruin things.

I asked him to describe some of the many important people he had met in the course of his thirty-six year broadcasting career.

CHARLES KURALT

In 1981 in Washington, D.C., I met Charles Kuralt when he received an award at the American Women in Radio and Television Conference I was attending with Kerry Callahan Bronson, radio broadcaster from Great Falls. Kuralt was one of my favorite broadcasters, known for his CBS *On the Road* series and as an anchor for the CBS Sunday morning news from 1979-1994. When I found out he liked to fly fish on the Big Hole River near Dillon, Montana, I sent him twenty of my husband's hand-tied flies. This was his response, dated June 8, 1981:

Dear Norma,
I'm forever opening packages, usually from PR men pushing some product. Yours is the first package in a long time that made my heart beat faster! How can I ever thank you for this king's ransom in flies? Your husband is a master tier. I couldn't tie flies like that if I lived to be a hundred. And you really didn't have to include an index to them. They are classics. I've already put them in a special Ashby box, in a special pocket in my vest, but I'm not sure whether I want to risk losing one in a Montana willow (my back casts lack a certain precision sometimes) or just keep them around for admiring. Tell your husband that I thank him, right down to the tips of my ten thumbs.
I expect I'll be in Montana this September. I haven't missed a September in some years. If I make it this year, I'll hope to see you!
Best, Charles Kuralt

Charles died in 1997 at the age of sixty-two.

They are all fascinating. I think Lyndon Johnson was one of the most fascinating men I ever met—especially trying to figure out what he was and how to get to know him. I think it was a tragedy in a way that the people of the United States never, I believe, did learn who the true Lyndon Johnson really was.

John F. Kennedy was very interesting. Jawaharlal Nehru was a fascinating human being. Charles deGaulle was interesting. They all have to be interesting to occupy their positions.

When I asked Chet how he met Tippy, he told me that she was the weather girl at the Washington, D.C. station where he worked. "Before we went on the air, I saw her in the studio," he said. "She accidentally walked in front of a camera. I asked David Brinkley to introduce us."

I asked Tippy to describe what for her were the highlights of Chet's career. She said that although political conventions had always been Chet's cup of tea, her favorite stories were his radio piece. "I love to listen to him do radio pieces," she said. "They are completely his."

Chet's memoir, *The Generous Years*, received such a wonderful reception around the country, especially in Montana, I asked him if he had plans to write another book.

"I have another book in me but book writing is the hardest work in the world," he answered. "You have to regiment yourself to your typewriter and commit to so many hours a day."

CLINT EASTWOOD

Clint Eastwood was in Great Falls shooting *Thunderbolt and Lightfoot* with Jeff Bridges in 1973. I interviewed him on location at what was then Hussman's Pool Hall (now Davidson Circle Plaza) on Central Avenue. Trying to seem relaxed in the presence of such a movie icon, I said to him as he stood with a cue stick in his hand by a pool table, "What's a nice guy like you doing is a place like this?"

He laughed and said, "We're shooting all kinds of scenes about playing pool."

"Are all these extras local people?" I asked.

Clint replied, "Yes, they hang out here."

Chet's second book, which he said would recap his years in broadcasting, was never written. He died four years after this interview. Here is a letter I received from Tippy at their home in Big Sky, dated May 1, 1974:

Dear Norma,

My heartfelt thanks to you for your warm and much appreciated letter, written more than a month ago. I know it will come as comforting news to you that Chet was working and stimulated until a few days before his death.

I plan to remain in Montana, living in this lovely home we built last year, probably going to work for Big Sky in time. I'm looking forward to it. Be assured that things are improving daily here, thanks to the likes of you.
With Love,
Tippy

Baroness Maria von Trapp

The Baroness Maria von Trapp, whose life was portrayed by Julie Andrews in the 1965 Academy-Award-winning movie, *The Sound of Music*, was in Great Falls for a Junior League Celebrity Series lecture. Prior to the movie, *The Sound of Music* appeared on Broadway, starring Mary Martin with music by Richard Rodgers and Oscar Hammerstein. I taped an interview with her that ran on our *Today in Montana* family Christmas show on December 24, 1968. On that same show, students from the C. M. Russell High School's production of *The Sound of Music* sang "Do-Re-Mi" and senior Karen Wraalstad, who played Mother Abbess, sang "Climb Every Mountain."

The Baroness appeared on the show in her native Austrian dirndl. At sixty-three years, she was agile, quick and very astute.

I opened the interview by asking the Baroness what she was doing now. She said that she lived in Stowe, Vermont, in a home called the Trapp Family Lodge.

> The little children from *The Sound of Music* have grown up. I have twenty-seven grandchildren. I am at the lodge in the winter and the summer. We have hired a ski instructor from Norway and have started a cross country ski school for people from eight to eighty. No excuse! In the summer, we have 180 flowerboxes at our lodge. We also have a gift shop with the lodge. I go to Europe once a year,

IRVING STONE

I interviewed Irving Stone in 1968 when he was promoting his book, *The Agony and the Ecstasy*, about the life of Michelangelo. He was very reserved and quite a challenge to interview. My forays into his life, his work and his family seemed to fall flat. I thought the interview was a flop until a fellow broadcaster from Great Falls, Audrey Creecy, (later Olson-Stratford) asked him a question that really cracked the ice with him, "Is it true, Mr. Stone," she said, "that the Sistine Chapel ceiling was really a paint-by-number?"

Norma and Baroness Maria von Trapp, whose life inspired *The Sound of Music*, and who was a Junior League Celebrity Series speaker in 1968.

especially Austria, and I pick handicrafts to sell. We also sell our books and records.

I asked the Baroness to describe for the audience her very interesting and varied life.

For two years, I tried very, very hard to become a nun. I didn't make it. But I learned the most important message and lesson for my whole life: to find out the will of God and then go and do it.

There came the moment when the Nazis were in Austria and my husband asked, "Do we want to keep our material goods? (We were rich people at the time, living on a big estate), or do we want to keep our spiritual goods?" he asked. "We can't have both any more."

We chose our spiritual goods, which meant that we had to secretly get out of Austria and flee. That made us refugees. That was in 1938. The people looked at us and said, "They are not Jewish. They wouldn't have to leave."

We went from country to country and turned our hobby of singing into a living. We saved every penny. We came to America and started our first concert tour. There were twelve in our family. We stood, we bowed and we sang. Our agent said something was missing in our performances but he didn't know what it was. We finally found out during a concert in Denver.

We were singing a folksong in which I had to take a deep breath and hold a note eight bars while my children were singing. In that crucial moment a fly was circling my face. I was too proper to bat it away. I took a deep breath and in went the fly! It's extremely difficult to choke in public gracefully. I was so upset about the whole thing. I thought I had let everybody down. I stepped forward and said to the audience, "What happened has never happened before. I just swallowed a fly!" The audience laughed; our family laughed. The ice was broken in our performance.

Later, when I asked her about the influence music has had on her life the Baroness talked about music as a universal language. "There's one song in *The Sound of Music*, 'Climb Every Mountain,' which almost became the Vermont National Anthem," she said.

She went on to comment about the times. It was 1968, the time when there were hippies and students were rioting or holding sit-ins to protest the Vietnam war. It was also a time when the United States was still engaged in fighting communism around the world.

> I'm asked what I think of the hippies, of the student riots. "What's to become of our youth?" people cry. "And communists? How will we ever lick them?" I really think instead of taking a stand against hippies and rioting students and communists, let's face them and learn about these phenomena.
>
> They are deficiencies, sicknesses in the body of our society. People talk, talk, talk and don't do anything about these deficiencies. Would it ever occur, for example, to anybody that the hippies and the rioting students of 1968 are the first generation of young people to be brought up by babysitters?

The Baroness went on to comment on

NORMAN VINCENT PEALE AND RUTH PEALE

Dr. Norman Vincent Peale and his wife Ruth were among my all time favorite guests. I interviewed the famous minister and author of *The Power of Positive Thinking* and his wife in the Great Falls International Airport when they were returning from a 1985 Farm Forum in Cut Bank where he had been the featured speaker.

When I asked Dr. Peale what advice he had to give someone who might be extremely discouraged and didn't see any light at the end of the tunnel, he said, "I would just apply what I apply to myself. I do my best and believe that with God's help the best will come. And I believe that if a person will pray and turn their problem over to the Lord and then try to follow his guidance, the sunshine will burst through the dark clouds."

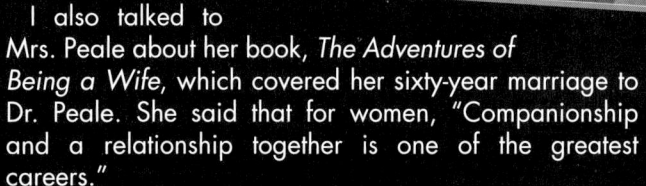

I also talked to Mrs. Peale about her book, *The Adventures of Being a Wife*, which covered her sixty-year marriage to Dr. Peale. She said that for women, "Companionship and a relationship together is one of the greatest careers."

I asked her if she felt that even though marriage is a partnership, so much is up to the woman. She leaned close to me and smiled. "Since you and I are women we can talk off the record," she said. "I think that women are smarter than men and I also think that they have a greater intuitive sensitivity. Study your man, because everybody has weaknesses and strengths. If a wife thinks she's going to change those weaknesses that won't happen. A young wife who read my book said she started to change herself and suddenly her husband changed too and she hadn't said a thing to him. Isn't that wonderful!"

67

how she felt that part of the cause for the student riots was that in American families more and more children were being raised by babysitters instead of mothers.

> When I first came to America thirty years ago, babysitting wasn't an institution—the babysitter came in and the mother went out. Young children, babies, need to be cuddled. No one watched these children grow up or cared. So now they come to college—these huge degree factories I call them. These professors have no feeling toward students. They are just numbers. Finally, these students have had enough.
>
> That's what started the student rioting in Berkeley. I was there two weeks later. I had heart-rending talks with students deep into the night. They were very serious and sincere young people. They are the only ones who speak up. It's a pity. We need to change some attitudes and get the mothers home.
>
> Let's do a little soul-searching. If you spend the first ten years with your children, they will spend the next ten years with you. You will need a blow torch to get them out of the house. Let's get the mothers home again and later when the kids are grown up, the mothers can go out and do all the interesting things that they want to do. But first there's no substitute for a mother.
>
> The hippies and the rioting, yelling students have so long missed personal attention and personal love, they just somehow create another group of people that care for them.

I asked her what we should turn to for new hope at this Christmas season.

Let's make this line from the song in *The Sound of Music* our theme song for 1969: "A song is no song til you sing it. A bell is no bell till you ring it. And love in your heart was not put there to stay. Love isn't love till you give it away (sic)."

The Baroness died in 1987 at the age of eighty-two. She is buried in Stowe, Vermont, next to her husband Georg von Trapp, who was a retired naval captain before he left Austria. Today, descendants of the Trapp Family Singers live in Montana's Flathead Valley and have given concerts around the state.

"Let's make this line from the song in The Sound of Music our theme song for 1969: 'A song is no song til you sing it. A bell is no bell till you ring it. And love in your heart was not put there to stay. Love isn't love till you give it away (sic).'"

Mary Kay Ash

At an American Women in Radio and Television national convention in San Francisco in 1982, I interviewed Mary Kay Ash, the founder and chairman of the board of Mary Kay Cosmetics. Mary Kay founded her company in September 1963, after she had retired from a lengthy and successful career in direct sales. It grew from her investment of $5,000 and nine saleswomen to an international organization of hundreds of thousands of beauty consultants and one-half billion dollars in sales in 1982.

I did the *Today in Montana* interview in a hotel suite at the convention site. Mary Kay was dressed in a beautiful pink ultra-suede suit. She wore gorgeous jewelry and her blonde hair and makeup were perfect. She was a walking advertisement for her cosmetics.

At that time, all of her products were in pink containers. I asked her if pink was her favorite color. "Not really," she said, and laughed. "In 1963, everyone had a pink bathroom." I perceived from her answer that her company made pink containers for her products to match everyone's pink bathrooms.

I then asked her to talk about the company's beginning. She noted that she started the company on Friday the 13th in 1963—which continued to be the company's "lucky number." It was a difficult time to start a company, she said, because society wasn't used to liberated women in 1963.

Mary Kay Ash, who founded Mary Kay Cosmetics, with Norma at the 1982 national convention of the American Women in Radio and Television in San Francisco.

> You walked two paces behind the boss and getting into the executive suite was out of the question. Since I had trained any number of men for those positions and then found them to be my superiors in a few months, I thought if I can train them, why can't I do that job? So when I retired I began thinking about writing a book to help women with some of the same obstacles I had encountered those twenty-five years I had worked.
>
> I wrote down all the problems and all the good things

about the companies where I had worked. When I got all these things on paper, I thought, wouldn't it be great if someone would do this instead of just talk about it?

Mary Kay Cosmetics was born.

Mary Kay had an unconventional approach to business. She considered the Golden Rule the founding principle of Mary Kay Cosmetics and the company's marketing plan was designed to allow women to advance by helping others to succeed. Unfailingly supportive and enthusiastic, she advocated "praising people to success." She encouraged people to succeed by saying, "If you think you can, you can. And if you think you can't, you're right." She also felt that "God came first, family second and career third," and she encouraged the women in her company to keep their lives balanced. She told me, "If you make all the money in the world but go home and have to count it all by yourself, and lose your family in the process, it's not worth it."

Mary Kay explained that each beauty consultant in her business is an independent contractor. Each contractor is president of her own company. There is no middle man. Consultants purchase the products directly from the company at a wholesale price and sell them to their clients at a retail price. They work at their own pace and on their own time. If they aspire to management, they can recruit others and build a team. That opens the way for top income, trips and prizes. The famous pink Cadillacs that her top salespeople earn are the most visible sign of success in the company.

Mary Kay went on to discuss the Mary Kay makeup.

PAT NIXON

When First Lady Pat Nixon came to Yellowstone National Park for the park's hundredth anniversary in 1972, reporters and cameramen were jammed around her so tightly I wasn't sure I could get near enough to ask her a question. When Secretary of the Interior Rogers Morton, who was accompanying her, saw my dilemma, he literally lifted me up and placed me in front of her.

My cameraman John Hildenstab was with me and we caught a few words with her on tape. "We've had a little rain, a little hail, a little wind," she said about her trip in her quiet, unassuming voice, "but it's been very pleasant and the warm-hearted people have made it so."

> I had been using this formula since the early 1950s. It's the best thing I've ever put on my face. I was able to buy the formula in 1963 and together with my marketing plan, I launched the company. I have often said, "When God made man, he was just practicing."

I asked her to explain the company's symbol— the bumble bee— which is used on jewelry earned by top performers.

> Aerodynamically the bumble bee's body is too heavy to fly but it doesn't know it, so it goes right on flying. I thought that's perfect. Women don't know how great they are. They really can fly.

The marketing plan for Mary Kay Cosmetics is known for its use of positive reinforcement. I asked her to describe why she came up with this positive sales model and what role praise has played in the success of her company.

> If there is a common denominator among women it is a lack of confidence in their own ability. If they will let go and use their innate ability to do all the things they like to do they can accomplish anything. We praise women to success.

I remarked that she appeared to be an ageless lady. Mary Kay reminded me that, at that time in 1982, she had sixteen grandchildren and four great-grandchildren. "Real beauty comes from within," she said. "If we can bring out a woman's inner beauty, all women are beautiful."

When I interviewed Mary Kay, I had no idea that one day I would become a Mary Kay beauty consultant. I know from experience that just a touch of lipstick, blush and mascara can make a big difference in how a woman looks and feels about herself. I had used the product for several years and liked it.

After I left KRTV in 1988, my consultant, Joanne Hinch, recruited me to take over some of her clients when she moved to Florida. I found myself in a whole new world of working for myself. I enjoyed selling cosmetics because every woman uses some form of cosmetics, whether it's a lipstick or the full skin care line and they need more when they run out. As Charles Russell writes in a chapter on fashions from his book *Trails Plowed Under*, "A woman can go farther with a lipstick than a man with a Winchester and a slab of bacon!"

"Real beauty comes from within," she said. "If we can bring out a woman's inner beauty, all women are beautiful."

Some of the highlights from my sixteen-year Mary Kay career include the following: I have been in the Queen's Court of Sales seven times. I visited Mary Kay's Dallas mansion and I sat in her pink bathtub, which was a tradition. I earned some sensational prizes for my sales performances, including diamond rings, fur coats, and three Grand Am Pontiacs. Most exciting of all, I had my name drawn for makeover photos that appeared on the inside cover page of the company magazine, *Applause*, in January 1992. I was a sales director for five years and built a team of wonderful women, but after attending twelve national seminars in Dallas and five leadership conferences, I decided I wanted more time to spend with my family and to pursue volunteer interests. I resigned my directorship and Caroline Sagunsky took over my team. I am still a beauty consultant and continue to enjoy using the products and serving my customers.

In my years of working for Mary Kay Cosmetics, I have most enjoyed hearing Mary Kay speak at seminars, talking to her at awards banquets and having my picture taken with her when I became a director. When she was talking to you, you felt like you were the only person in the room. She had these memorable sayings: "Pretend that every single person you meet has a sign around his or her neck that says, 'Make me feel important.' Not only will you succeed in sales, you will succeed in life. God didn't have

ROY ROGERS

Roy Rogers, the feature act at the Montana State Fair in 1969. Rogers was accompanied by his wife, Dale Evans. Great Falls went wild at the appearance of the king and queen of the cowboy set. Rogers was just as genuine, down-to-earth and funny in person as he is on the screen.

time to make a nobody, only a somebody. I believe that each of us has God-given talents within us waiting to be brought to fruition."

Mary Kay suffered a stroke in 1996 and died on November 22, 2001. She was eighty-three. Her son, Richard Rogers, took over as CEO of the company and today Mary Kay Cosmetics has 1,300,000 representatives world-wide. At the end of 2003, the company had $3.6 billion in retail sales and for the eleventh year in a row, it has been rated number one in skin care and cosmetics sales.

Arlene Francis

In May 1987, Arlene Francis, radio and television personality, stage and screen actress, author and lecturer, was in Great Falls to lecture for the Senior Care Program of the Montana Deaconess Medical Center. Arlene was well-known for the popular television show *What's My Line?* She appeared on the show live and in syndication for twenty-five years. As a panelist, she was blindfolded and had to guess the interesting or unusual occupations of the guests by asking yes or no questions about them. Famous guests as well as regular citizens tried to stump the panel. In the 1950s, she was one of the most active women in television, sometimes appearing on all three networks in the same week. Arlene was the first woman to host a network television magazine show in the 1950s. On July 19, 1954, she appeared on the cover of *Newsweek*, which hailed her as the first woman of television.

I had watched Arlene on *What's My Line?* when I was a young woman. I remembered how glamorous, witty and warm she was. She had all of those qualities when I met her in person.

When I interviewed her for *Today in Montana*, she had just finished lecturing to an auditorium full of people. In her lecture titled "The Prime of Our Life," she advised senior citizens to "throw away the rule book because it is never too late" to live a full and interesting life. I asked her to elaborate.

She tossed back her hair and laughed. "If you manage to keep

Actress and broadcaster Arlene Francis, who was interviewed by Norma in 1987.

WALTER BRENNAN

I met character actor Walter Brennan on location at the Little Bighorn Battlefield in southwestern Montana in the summer of 1965. He was there doing a special for NBC's *Project 20*. I was there to do a show on the making of a documentary. He was very accommodating and after the filming, I received these two letters from him from his home in Moorpark, California:

The letter, dated August 5, 1965 reads:

Dear Norma,
That Montana sun and those reflectors did not do me any good. The second day after I got home my face broke out with sun poisoning, and I was confined to the house for about a week.
  Hope the show turns out as well as they expected.
  It was nice meeting and talking to you.
  Best to you and yours
  Sincerely
  Walter Brennan

Dated Aug. 29, 1965

Dear Norma,
  I have been intending to write and thank you for the birthday card and the pictures you so kindly sent me.
  I was up in New England from Aug. 12 to the 20th. Went up to Salem, Mass. for the Heritage Parade on the 15th. Terribly hot and humid, but we have had our share of that here.
  We start our pilot for the new TV show Horatio Alger Jones *tomorrow and will be on that for a week. I just hate to be idle. You'd think at 71, I'd go lie down some place.*
  Have a starting date of October 4th on the show (feature) for Walt Disney The Gnomobile, *which will probably take 3 or 4 months. Happier when I'm working.*
  Many thanks again for the card and pictures. I think the pictures came out fine.
  Best to you and yours,
  Walter

74

your eyes open and your heart open, there's lots to do and to see," she said. "Sometimes it gets better."

I then asked her to comment on the older women that we were seeing more often in the media—women such as Angela Lansbury in *Murder, She Wrote* and Barbara Walters on *20/20*, who were both in their 50s.

"You can still be gorgeous at fifty, sixty, seventy or eighty," she said. "Women are taking better care of themselves and are looking more attractive."

I asked her to describe her television interview with Helen Keller, the author and lecturer who was blind and deaf from the age of two and was taught sign language by her teacher and lifelong companion Annie Sullivan—a story that was made famous in the play, *The Miracle Worker*.

> She was a guest on my show called *Home*. Her companion [Annie Sullivan] would talk into her hand. She had learned to say a few things. As I spoke to her she put her fingers to my lips. She had also learned to lip read by feeling.

Arlene said she asked Helen, through Annie Sullivan, if she could have only one of her senses—hearing, seeing, speech—which one she would want the most.

"Oh, it would be hearing," Helen had replied. "I would want to be able to hear music, to hear the sound of children laughing, to hear the people that I love talk to me."

I asked Arlene to describe what it was like appearing for all those years on *What's My Line?*

> The show was always live except when it was in syndication. Ronald Reagan, when he was an actor, Bob Hope and Gary Cooper were among our many guests. They never made more than $50 for their appearance and then only if they won. It was terrific to be paid for having a good time at a party.

I asked her how she had been able to balance a very successful career and her long-standing marriage to Actor Martin Gabel as well as her role as a mother to her son.

> I think loving does everything for you, as well as affec-

"You can still be gorgeous at fifty, sixty, seventy or eighty," she said. "Women are taking better care of themselves and are looking more attractive."

tion and honesty and understanding and compromise—all those good words. If you can live with them long enough and not get too mad too many times, I think you can have a very happy life. I have certainly had that.

I asked her to describe a book she had written titled, *That Certain Something: The Magic of Charm.*

I thought about how people can be more thoughtful and understanding and how important it is to listen. I wrote to people and asked them their definition of charm. Mrs. Eleanor Roosevelt wrote back, "I found it difficult to find one word but the word that means the most to me is kindness."

When I asked Arlene what she would most like to be remembered for, she smiled and said quietly, "I would like to be remembered as a good wife and a good mother and not a bad actress."

I remarked on Arlene's diamond heart necklace, which was her trademark on *What's My Line?* The necklace was given to her by her husband and was unique because there were diamonds on both sides of the heart.

Arlene fingered the necklace. "Yes," she said. "I wear it every day. I have it on now."

I told Arlene that my mother was so inspired by seeing her necklace on *What's My Line?* that she requested one, with diamonds on just one side, from my stepfather.

Arlene was eighty-nine when we did this interview. She died in 2001 at the age of ninety-three. Following her death, her son gave this tribute to her, saying, "My mother was a wonderful, loving woman who was able to communicate her warmth and vitality to millions of people as well as to my father and me."

—3—
On Camera: Montanans

Although my celebrity guests were exciting to meet and interview, the majority of my 26,000 guests over the years were Montanans. I have always been in awe of the human spirit and people who do interesting things with their lives, whether it be a job, a talent, a project, a worthy cause, or people who are articulate about an issue. To that end, I had Montanans from all walks of life, from school principals to singers, from homemakers to snake handlers.

I am a fourth generation Montanan. I have lived here all but seven years of my life and I have a basic love and appreciation for the people of this state. I also have had a deep interest in the history of our state, which is why I wrote and produced documentaries about state history such as *Last Chance Gulch,* the 1964 celebration of Helena's centennial, and *First Ladies of Montana* in 1986.

Those first few weeks, my guests were primarily from Great Falls, such as the guest on our second show, Leroy Stahl, an expert on publicity, who gave tips on how to work with the media. Others during that early time were Chris Stevens, who discussed what it meant to be a Democrat, and Bill Baillie, who discussed what it meant to be a Republican.

Because of the magazine format of the show, many of our interviews were public service in nature, promoting everything from a threshing bee to a school play. Viewers were among my best suppliers of guests, as they would let me know about an interesting person in their families or community or a cause or project I should be promoting. Before long, guests on the show were not just from Great Falls, but from around Montana, the nation and the world.

In 1964, for example, 1,046 guests appeared from forty-eight Montana towns, nineteen states and eleven foreign countries. Our most ambitious program that year was the performance by the Montana Centennial Band—all seventy-six members played their

---

I am a fourth-generation Montanan. I have lived here all but seven years of my life and I have a basic love and appreciation for the people of this state.

MARTHA BURKE of Stevensville, Montana, was chosen not only Montana Mother of the Year, but National Mother of the Year in 1985. A remarkably small woman with snow white hair, a ready smile and a mischievous sparkle in her eyes, Martha had raised twelve children. Some of her comments were so hilarious I found myself laughing out loud. She told me that when her husband of forty-seven years heard of her award, he said, "How am I going to live with you now?"

When I asked her how she coped with such a large family, she replied, "The children didn't all come at once. After the first two they started helping with the rest."

Martha had this advice for young mothers. "Remember, motherhood is a lifetime commitment," she said. "If you don't have to work, stay home so you won't miss those baby days." She said she survived the years of raising children with a philosophy she developed when she was visiting the dentist. When she told him how much she dreaded the drill, he said, "This too shall pass." She said those four words helped her more than anything else with the challenges in her life.

At the time I interviewed her, Martha had twenty grandchildren and one great-grandchild. "It's fun to be a grandparent," she said. "You don't have all the responsibility."

---

instruments in the field behind KRTV. Later, in that same field, we featured a demonstration of the Blackfeet riding games of O-Mok-See with ten horses and riders.

Television was still so new in those early days that people were excited to be on the air with me. I never begged anyone to be on because if they were uncomfortable about it they would not have made a good guest. I usually booked guests weeks in advance, but one morning in 1965 our guest didn't show up. My musician, Lou Bryant, and I ad-libbed and then I interviewed our engineer, our cameraman and our salesman, and we kept the show rolling. Fortunately that didn't happen often as free airtime was at a premium and the majority of our guests kept their appointments.

I wrote a tribute to Montanans for the twentieth anniversary show of *Today in Montana* that expresses my love for, admiration of, and pride in the people of Montana—for their courage, their strength and their endless variety. I compiled two essays I had written, "What Is a Montanan?" and "The Montana Woman" into one, titled "Montanans," and Denys Taiple of Great Falls calligraphed it. I had one thousand printed, courtesy of the Montana Power Company for our viewers. I had one copy framed and it is still hangs in our home, a fond memory of my time with *Today in Montana*.

Montanans
by Norma Ashby

What are Montanans? You might say we are a special breed of people.

We come from pioneer stock that has given us strength to face the perils of these troubled times.

We're proud of our rich heritage and the sacrifices our ancestors made that benefit us today.

We're unimpressed with pretense.

Montanans are among the friendliest people you'll ever meet.

We enjoy showing our state to visitors.

We're sports-minded. We're fishermen, hunters, skiers, swimmers, backpackers.

Montanans delight in exploring this big country we call home.

You'll find us on the most remote mountain peak, on the lake, the stream and on the prairie.

We appreciate the outdoors and see the preservation of its beauty as a personal responsibility so that our children and our children's children can enjoy it as much as we do.

Montanans know the importance of a strong family life.

We know the land, the joy of planting crops and seeing their successful yield.

We know livestock and the satisfaction that comes with a good price at market.

Montanans are writers, artists, musicians, sculptors, potters who are inspired by our environment to create beauty.

We believe in good education and know that real education is a lifelong process.

We are characters who have funny stories to tell.

Montanans are young people, eager to have their say.

Adventurous in spirit, constantly seeking new experiences, we love to travel, always happy to return to our Montana home.

We realize our profits might be bigger someplace else but we prefer our way of life in Montana to finding riches elsewhere.

Montanans know wealth is not measured in gold and silver but in peace with our Creator and in harmony with our fellow man.

True Montanans believe that along with the state's mountains, sky, streams, forests, minerals, air and wildlife, the human beings who live here with us have the potential to become Montana's greatest natural resource.

Montana's Governors

During my years on *Today in Montana*, I visited with many governors of the state, from the friendly Tim Babock to the articulate Forrest Anderson, from the popular Tom Judge to the down-to-earth Ted Schwinden. Whether Republican or Democrat, conservative or liberal, the governors of our state have been an interesting and varied group of people.

During my years on Today in Montana, I visited with many governors of the state, from the friendly Tim Babock to the articulate Forrest Anderson, from the popular Tom Judge to the down-to-earth Ted Schwinden

> "True Montanans believe that along with the state's mountains, sky, streams, forests, minerals, air and wildlife, the human beings who live here with us have the potential to become Montana's greatest natural resource."

Governor Tim Babcock, a Republican from Glendive, served as governor from 1962 to 1969, during which time he presided over the Montana Territorial Centennial Celebration in 1964. He and his wife Betty led the Montana delegation to the New York World's Fair and they were excellent ambassadors of goodwill for the state. He was open and friendly and very approachable as governor. I enjoyed working on his Centennial Commission with people like Chairman L.W. "Uppie" Upshaw from Great Falls, who taught me how to put on a successful celebration.

Governor Forrest Anderson, a Democrat from Helena who served from 1969 to 1972, was a man I had known since growing up in Helena. I babysat his three small children, Marjorie, Newell and Arlee, when I was thirteen. When he was governor, he and his wife Evelyn would reminisce about the times I took care of his children. He came to our KRTV studios to be interviewed by the League of Women Voters during his race for the governor's office in 1968. In 1970, he designated me his Ambassador of Goodwill to the International Convention of Women in Radio and Television in London. A handsome, silver-haired man who was a former attorney general, he was a smooth and articulate politician.

Governor Tom Judge was a Democrat from Helena who was in the governor's office from 1973 to 1980. He was also a 1953 classmate of mine at Helena High School. Tom went to Notre Dame, served in the state legislature and was the first governor of my generation. His mother, Blanche Judge, had taught social dancing to my friends and me when we were in grade school. I covered Tom's inaugural ball at the Civic Center in Helena and enjoyed talking to him, his wife Carol, and his mother at the ball. As the youngest governor and first lady in Montana, they made a very attractive couple.

Governor Ted Schwinden, a Democrat from Wolf Point, served as governor in 1981, and he was reelected in 1984. By 1988, he decided not to run for reelection because he wanted to spend more time with his family. When I interviewed him for *Today in Montana*, he said the major change in the Montana economy was that we were seeing a shift from basic industries to service industries. "Mining, manufacturing, timber, transportation are all losing jobs," he said. "These are opportunities for taking action and taking risks."

He added, "I can't grow up as a farm kid in Montana and not take some risks. I have awakened every morning since 1981 excited to go to work. After the November election, however, I have no intention of seeking public office. Jean and I may help out with our family farm near Wolf Point. The life of a politician is more difficult for the family than for the politician. They pay a larger personal price than the office holder."

When I asked him what First Lady Jean Schwinden's role had been, the Governor said, "She has an exquisite ability to perceive what other Montanans perceive. She is a great reader of our proposals."

He said the thing he was proudest of during his term, was carrying every county in Montana in the 1984 election and winning his first term in the legislature in 1958. "I got elected by my neighbors, the people who knew me best," he said. "That was tremendously rewarding. I have enjoyed being governor. I think people have felt at ease talking with me. The most frustrating thing about my office is having to wear a tie."

Governor Schwinden was one of Montana's most popular governors, appealing to both Democrats and Republicans. He was very down to earth and insisted on answering the phone in the Governor's Mansion when he was home. Once when I called the mansion and he answered, I was so flabbergasted, I said, "I didn't expect to get you, Governor." He replied, "Why not? I live here."

IVAN DOIG

One of Montana's most successful writers, Ivan Doig is a guest I marveled at each time I interviewed him. He was so gifted with words and characters and descriptions, I found myself rereading passages when I finished reading his books. This was particularly true of his first book, *This House of Sky*, which was published in 1978.

The book was a memoir, tracing his coming of age in the country around White Sulphur Springs, with his father and grandmother and then moving to the Rocky Mountain Front and the communities of Dupuyer and Valier. The book captured the hearts of not only Montanans but of readers of good writing everywhere. Nominated for the National Book Award, *This House of Sky* is still in print and continues to be one of the best books written about Montana.

On top of being an exceptional writer, Ivan is an exceptional person. He and his wife Carol, who helps him do research for his writing, are a devoted and friendly couple who always make you feel they are glad to see you whether it's on a TV show or at a book signing.

Books on tape by authors can be especially appealing and no author reads his own works better than Ivan. *This House of Sky* and *English Creek* are two which have brought me great pleasure, especially when I am driving the long distance under the big sky between Great Falls and Browning in the country portrayed so beautifully through Ivan's writing.

Since I left *Today in Montana* in 1988, three more people have served as governor.

Stan Stephens, a Republican from Havre, served from 1989 to 1992. He was the first broadcaster to be in that position. Stan had the distinction of serving during the Montana Statehood Centennial Year in 1989 and welcoming President George H. W. Bush onto the grounds of the State Capitol. He and his wife Ann were right at home in the Governor's Mansion and made sure Elsie Jones, who had cooked for seven Montana governors and their families, had a remodeled kitchen.

Governor Marc Racicot, a Republican from Libby and another former attorney general, served for two terms, from 1993 to 2000. A slim, sandy-haired and energetic man, Racicot was another of Montana's most popular governors. He and his wife Theresa, with their five children, made a lively household at the Governor's Mansion. Marc, a friend of George W. Bush when he was governor of Texas, was appointed by President Bush to be his campaign chairman for the 2004 presidential election. One of our most personable governors, he has made numerous appearances on national radio and television.

Governor Judy Martz, a Republican from Butte, served from 2000 to 2004. Judy was our first woman governor. A tall, platinum blonde, former Olympic speed skater, she has served with grace in the state's most demanding political position and has received enough awards and gifts to fill a museum. Her symbol has been the turtle—an animal that she says only moves ahead when he sticks his neck out. She had a turtle pin created, which she has given out by the thousands. A highlight of her term was the Centennial

CLAIRE DEL GUERRA, who was the Cascade County home demonstration agent off and on from 1956 to the present, probably made more appearances on *Today in Montana* than any other guest. Claire shared her wealth of knowledge on a wide variety of subjects, from making placemats with used greeting cards to creating delicious ethnic dishes, such as her grandmother's ravioli. She organized all the food demonstrations during the State Fair and provided free recipes for our viewers. She had and still has a natural rapport with people. She had a strong following among our large audience of homemakers, who looked forward to her regular appearances. Her hearty laugh, tireless work ethic and love of people have endeared her to all who know her. She will always remind me of the "Energizer bunny" who is going strong and who leaves wide smiles in her wake.

of the State Capitol in 2002, when she was the parade marshal. During that celebration I was her guest at the mansion. Among the many personal things she showed me was the bedspread her sister made for her from T-shirts she had been given by individuals and causes. Judy is looking forward to spending more time with her husband, Harry, her two children and her grandchild. She is also planning to do some motivational speaking.

Montana's First Ladies

In 1986 and in 1996, I interviewed the seven living first ladies of Montana. These interviews ran in primetime specials on the Montana Television Network. I asked each first lady what advice she would have to give a woman who might someday be first lady. Here are their replies:

Maxine Nutter Larson, 1961 to 1962, said, "Don't take the job as seriously as I think I did."

Betty Babcock, 1962 to 1969, suggested that a first lady should get right to work. "If you don't begin you can never win," she said. "Live each day as it comes. It's an experience a woman shouldn't pass up. And of course she should support her husband in any way she can."

Evelyn Anderson, 1969 to 1973, said that she found that if "you were kind to people, you'll find it comes back to you many times."

Carol Judge, 1973 to 1980, said, "Enjoy that time because it's brief."

Jean Schwinden, 1981 to 1988, advised future first ladies to think of themselves as "tenants of the Governor's Mansion. Time goes very quickly. Enjoy it while you have the opportunity. Not very many people have this opportunity."

Ann Stephens, 1989 to 1992, said that "you can make the job what you want it to be."

Theresa Racicot, 1993 to 2000, advised, "Be yourself. Have fun. You can't take it too seriously."

Elsie Jones, who cooked for seven Montana governors and their families, said this about her job: "I have been very happy and very fortunate. I love the first ladies. We all got along fine. They never

First Lady Carol Judge in 1974 receiving the first sheet of Easter Seals from Norma, Honorary Easter Seal Chairman at the Governor's Mansion in Helena.

VIVIAN PALADIN was the editor of the *Montana Magazine of Western History* from 1966 to 1978 and, in my opinion, was one of the magazine's finest editors. I interviewed her about her "Women and the American West" issue in the summer of 1974 and again in 1978 when she retired. When I asked if she would be Sacagawea if she could have been anyone in Montana history, she laughed.

"Hell no," she replied. "I'd be Lewis or Clark."

Born in Glasgow, Montana, the second of six daughters, this tall pretty woman with a great sense of humor and a journalism background came to the Montana Historical Society in 1956. Vivian's understanding of visual presentation and writing helped double the magazine's circulation and made it a widely imitated journal. Her tireless efforts on behalf of the magazine and historical society garnered her awards from the National Press Woman's Association, National Cowboy Hall of Fame, American Association for State and Local History, and the Western Historical Association. Her own publications included *Helena: An Illustrated History* with Jean Baucus in 1983 and *E. E. Heikka: Sculptor of the American West* in 1980.

I was mistress of ceremonies at Vivian's retirement mini-roast in Helena on August 26, 1979 and had the privilege of introducing the speaker, Dorothy Johnson, the author of *The Hanging Tree* and *The Man Who Shot Liberty Valance*, both of which were made into movies. Dorothy produced a list of fictitious articles that she claimed Vivian had refused to run. These included titles such as "My Life As an Evangelist" by Harvey Logan, alias Kid Curry, and "The Handy Guide to Human Anatomy," by Liver-Eating Johnson.

When Vivian died in 2002, there were many tributes to her skill and her intelligence, but this is my favorite. Ellen Baumler, an interpretive historian at the Montana Historical Society said, "Vivian cared deeply about bringing Montana history to Montanans...she paved the way for those of us women who write about history. Although her epitaph may simply read 'Vivian Paladin, 1918-2002,' what she accomplished in that dash between the dates was most remarkable."

spoke a cross word to me. I really feel that the State of Montana should be proud of their first ladies because they really have done a lot for the state."

J. K. Ralston

In August 1970, I interviewed my good friend J. K. "Ken" Ralston, cowboy, artist, poet, and writer from Billings whom I had met with his wife Willo during the Montana Territorial Centennial Celebration in 1964. He was on *Today in Montana* to promote his new book, *Rhymes of a Cowboy*, his collection of poems, stories, sketches and paintings that he dedicated "to the cowboys I knew and rode with, and to the old-timers whose tales of the early West I listened to as a boy."

A tall, lean, kindly man, who always dressed in western clothes, Ken was one of the last of the cowboy painters who had experienced the West first-hand. His parents came to Alder Gulch in 1864 and to Last Chance Gulch in 1865. In 1878, his father moved his cattle from the Prickly Pear Valley to the Teton River near Choteau, where Ken was born in 1896. He worked as a cowboy for the old 79, the CK, the F- and others. Through his brush and pen he shared his personal experiences of the West he loved for all of us to enjoy.

We talked about some of his best known historical paintings, including *Into the Unknown* which depicts Lewis and Clark meeting the Shoshone Indians at Camp Fortunate at the head of the Beaverhead River. The painting currently hangs in the Jefferson National Expansion Memorial in St. Louis. His paintings *Call of the Bugle* and *After the Battle*—depicting the battle between Custer's Seventh Cavalry and the Sioux and Cheyenne warriors—hangs in the visitors' center at the Little Bighorn Battlefield National Monument near Hardin.

I asked Ralston to read his poem, "Idols of a Boy." He said the

Norma and J.K. Ralston, who discussed his book, *Rhymes of a Cowboy* in 1970.

poem was a tribute to two of Montana's greatest men, cowboy artist Charlie Russell and poet Wallace Coburn:

> Idols of a Boy
> By J.K. Ralston
>
> The cowboy was my hero
> When I was just a kid.
> To me romance and glamour shone
> On everything he did;
> But of all those lusty heroes,
> The two outstanding men
> Were Russell with his brushes
> And Coburn with his pen.

In the centerfold of the book is a painting *The Old 79*, which accompanies this long poem which he shared with me.

> Day Herding in the Rain
> By J.K. Ralston
>
> The water's trickling off my hat,
> My slicker's dripping too;
> The muffler 'round my neck is wet,
> My boots are leaking through.
> I sit and freeze and cuss and wait—
> A minute seems a day.
> Day herdin's something I sure hate
> When days are damp and grey.
>
> A cold mist settles in the bend,
> 'Nigh blotting out the hill.
> The rain continues to descend,
> The air is raw and chill.
> I wish I had a cigarette,
> But with fingers stiff and dead,
> I couldn't roll one on a bet
> And so I cuss instead.
>
> My horse stands humped with tail a-drip,
> As if he were in pain,
> The water's trickling off his hip

A tall, lean, kindly man, who always dressed in western clothes, Ken was one of the last of the cowboy painters who had experienced the West first-hand.

And streaming from his mane.
He looks almighty some forlorn
With winkers dripping tears.
I bet he wisht he's never born
To follow up the steers.

The cattle crowd the coulee sides,
A-hidin' from the blow;
They stand about with rain-soaked hides
And voice a tale of woe.
Across the creek against a hill
And backed up to a tree,
A-top his horse sets Dogie Bill,
No doubt as cold as me.

The lucky hands are in the camp,
A dry and cozy place.
Ringed around a tarp with legs a-cramp,
All prayin' for an ace.
But me, I sit and groan and freeze
And call myself a name
For cottonin' to this cowboy wheeze
and following the game.

Somewhere I read, we make our bed;
I reckon this is right.
At times life's mostly in the red,
Again it's rosy bright.
We all, I 'spose must have our woes
And bear our share of pain.
There comes a time for all of us
To day herd in the rain.

And so it goes, least I suppose
From the border to the line.
There's them that gets the toughest rows
And luck like this is mine.
For me, I'm that unlucky bird
When days are chill and damp
It comes my turn to go on herd
While others lay in camp.

IRA PERKINS,
a rancher in Teton County, was the principal and a teacher at Bynum School in Bynum, Montana, when I interviewed him in 1953. He was celebrating his fiftieth year at the school. For Ira, teaching was more an avocation than a vocation. He had a great time, he told me, teaching school.

He also had the most unique approach to education I had ever seen. He made sure that his students could dance, do gymnastics and play a musical instrument in addition to learning the basics of English, math, science and history.

We went on location to the Bynum school and I marveled at Ira and his student body. All of the students were on the dance floor—from first to eighth graders—doing every dance step Ira could teach them, from the polka to the waltz. First graders danced with fifth graders; eighth graders danced with second graders. It was great to see such camaraderie—and dance was a great way to build the kids' self-confidence.

Ira told us that when these students graduated and went to Choteau High School, they were among the most popular kids in school because they could all dance. He said they were whizzes in music too, because they had been exposed to music at such an early age.

Charles Kuralt of CBS featured Ira and his students on his *On the Road* series in 1986, when Ira was named the longest-tenured teacher at the same school in the United States.

"Some of the brands in the painting—and of course these are only a few that were on that range—are the 79, the CK, and the N-, and the H+. Those were all outfits that had a lot of cattle on the range at that time."

I asked him to talk about the brands on the cattle in the painting.

The old 79 was a well-known cow outfit in Montana. They started out on the Marias River in 1879, moved over to the Musselshell, and then finally they had one outfit on the Big Dry, the area between the Yellowstone and Musselshell rivers, where I rode for them.

DZ was the brand on old Dan Zimmerman's steers. He was a big cattleman in North Dakota and he had brought up these Texas longhorns on the Rosebud River and in the spring they would bring them north of the river and make a deal with the 79 to ship the cattle. They were plenty wild and scary and we had a lot of trouble with them.

Some of the brands in the painting—and of course these are only a few that were on that range—are the 79, the CK, and the N-, and the H+. Those were all outfits that had a lot of cattle on the range at that time.

This painting is a self-portrait. I wrote the poem first and then made the painting in 1959.

I told him, "You can just feel the cold and wet in that painting. I guess it was a pretty miserable job." He agreed. Then he went on to explain that the horse was one of the day herding ponies that we used to call a cow horse.

I then asked him if he preferred night herding to day herding.

The night herding could be disagreeable but your shift was much shorter. The middle of the night would be an hour and a half. Day herding started at daylight if you were on the morning shift and you didn't get off until 11:30 a.m. when you were relieved. In the afternoon the hours were long, especially if the weather was bad. I think every cowpuncher has had that experience of sitting there, freezing in the rain. You get so you can't even roll a cigarette. If you try to, the water drips off your hat and your fingers are cold.

I asked Ken if the book was something he had dreamed about doing for a long time.

I started to write some of the poems thirty years ago and some of my sketches were done then, so I finally decided to make a book out of them. It was published by the

Rimrock Publishing Company in Billings, an enterprise of Frank Cross, a wonderful man.

On the back of Ken's book is a color picture of his studio in Billings. When I asked him if he sketched his works first on location and then came back to the studio to paint them, Ken said he did. "I actually sketch with a brush," he said. "I find more freedom that way."

When I asked him to describe his art training, he said that he didn't have too much. "I attended the Chicago Art Institute two different times," he said and laughed. "I got some ideas and enjoyed myself, but actual experience is the best teacher. Experience, practice, and observation make an artist out of you."

Maida McCartney

In 1975 I interviewed Maida McCartney, who hosted the daily *Chinook Hour* radio program for nearly two decades over KOJM in Havre. She remains one of the most outstanding Montana radio broadcasters, who provided the eyes and ears for an audience that stretched across the "Hi-Line" of northern Montana. Maida was chosen as one of fifty pioneer broadcasters in the nation to be included in an oral history project for the Broadcast Pioneers Library in Washington, D. C.

Maida was a tall, stately woman with glasses and gray hair. She was outgoing and friendly and had a hearty laugh. She loved people. She had four children and ten grandchildren and her family, friends and her listening audience were very important to her. I visited her once in the upstairs room in her home where she broadcast her radio show. I was very impressed with her radio work, even more so after I interviewed her.

Maida began as a reporter for the *Chinook Opinion*, where for years she had a column called "The Sugar City Silhouettes." She got her start in radio in 1946, and moved to KOJM in 1947. She said the idea for a radio show came when her daughter, a script writer for the local radio station KAVR, was discussing the idea for a program with Ed Lovelace. Maida said she suggested doing something called the *Chinook Hour*.

> I never thought of doing it myself. I was only going to write the news for it. Ed said, "All right, you go ahead and write the news." They sold out before I really got my feet on the ground. KOJM credits me with nineteen years. I really had twenty years on radio because I was with KAVR for a while.

"I got some ideas and enjoyed myself, but actual experience is the best teacher. Experience, practice and observation make an artist out of you."

When I asked her where she had her first broadcast, she laughed. "I broadcast from the Juline International Harvester Building on Highway 2 just outside of Chinook," she said. "They had an air-tight, noise-tight cubicle and it was hotter than a firecracker."

Maida said she took over the program when Lyle Leeds, who formerly had the show, was too tired to read the news.

> One day he said, "Why don't you do it?" So I just picked up the news and talked to our various merchants and kidded them along the way. I told my listeners, "The story goes that Will Rogers said he never met a man he didn't like. That is not true. He never kidded a man he didn't like. So I told the various merchants that if I kidded them along the way, they'd know it was because I liked them. "If I don't kid you," I told them. "I don't like you." So everybody wanted to be kidded.
>
> Then the sponsors kept calling Lyle and suggesting that he let me do the news program. When they asked me if I would take it over, I said, "I'll have to talk to my family and my husband and see, because if I take it, I will keep it. I won't just let it go by the boards. Give me twenty-four hours to think it over, because it's going to mean a change in our whole regime. We'll move the station down to the west window in my home so I can go up the long flight of stairs and look out over the prairie that I love.

Broadcaster Maida McCartney with Norma at KOJM radio in Havre in 1975.

Maida said when her daughter left home, she turned her bedroom into a studio, and the whole family agreed to help her out if she took the show. "If it hadn't been for their continued support and kindly understanding and the wonderful way that all my hometown greeted me and took care of things for me, I never could have done it alone," she said.

For the next nineteen years, Maida's *Chinook Hour* was narrated from the bedroom in her home, as Maida overlooked her beloved prairie. Her theme song for all those years was "Dear Hearts and Gentle People," which Bing Crosby sent her. "I didn't want anybody else's record but Bing's," she said, "because he could do it better than anyone."

Maida had told me she had interviewed more than 3,000 guests, so I asked her to describe some of the people she interviewed on the show.

> We had exchange students from Scotland, Ireland, Sweden, Denmark, Norway, Turkey and Italy along with other people that registered as they came in. We kept track of over 3,000 and I'm sure there were returns that we didn't even bother to write down.

I asked Maida if she ever had any hesitation about inviting strangers into her home and up that long flight of stairs into her bedroom. She laughed heartily and told me this story.

> Herb De Bries, bless his heart, used to come running up at the last minute with some news items and sometimes make quite a racket. KOJM told me there was too much background noise in my house so I put a note on the door, "Please do not ring the bell. Come in quietly during the broadcast."
>
> There was a fella who was in his cups a little too much. He came to the door, read the note and walked up the stairs. He saw me sitting there looking out the west window and giving the news and he said, "What're ya doin', talk'n to yourself, all by yourself up here?" So I called Jim Sanger, who was on the other side of the board (in the control room at KOJM) in Havre, and I said, "Jim, put on a record. We've got a little difficulty here." I led the man downstairs, gave him some money to go downtown and eat and locked the door.

I asked Maida to describe the format of *The Chinook Hour*.

> I had all these sponsors and that's another story. Those sponsors were wonderful. If I didn't want to advertise prunes or bananas or strawberries or something—if that

"We'll move the station down to the west window in my home so I can go up the long flight of stairs and look out over the prairie that I love."

got tiresome—I just didn't advertise them. I just went on with something that was interesting and gave the credit to the man that owned the business, whether it was groceries or meats. They used to tie me up on fresh sliced sidepork. You try and say that real fast.

Maida said she did not have to solicit her own sponsors, the station took care of that. "Mostly sponsors called in and wanted to get on," she said. "And they got on."

I pointed out that she was playing a very vital communication role in a small community because at that time there were no rural telephones or television. I asked her to expand on some of the services a local radio show had to provide.

> The ranchers and farmers say it was invaluable because of the services that we gave through the help of the county officials—the police department and the men from the county roads, for example. We were told officially exactly what roads were open so that cattle could be fed and all the things that were possible given the road conditions. Then the police department always kept me informed, so everything that I put on the program came from the best authority I could get.
>
> During the heavy snows there was a man who came from Helena one night and called the McCartney residence, thinking he was getting my son Clay, who had something to do with getting the heavy equipment in for snow. He said to me, "Is this the McCartney's?" I said, "Yes." He said, "I just got into town with a big weasel and two cats. What do ya want me to do?"
>
> At that time, I had been telling my listeners to feed their animals because they were hungry and the snow was deep. Thinking he was referring to that, I said, "Well, if you think I'm going to get up at two o'clock in the morning and feed your weasel and cats, you're crazy. Feed them yourself!" He laughed and laughed and told everybody in town that I didn't know what heavy snow removal equipment was!

When I asked her to describe the greatest catastrophe that she'd helped her readers through, she didn't hesitate. "It was the floods," she answered. "The floods of 1952 and the snows of '52 and '55. We had a devastating flood in our valley that people just barely recovered from.

I asked her if the station gave her any kinds of restrictions on what she could broadcast. Did she have complete freedom to put on the program whatever she wanted, or did the management of KOJM ever call her and tell her they didn't want her to touch this or that subject?

> They trusted me and shivered in their shoes. I assure you, they had many anxious moments, but I tried to stay within the right things to do and say. I didn't want to embarrass anybody or anything and I never did to my knowledge in any way injure or hurt anyone at any time. When I announced anybody that had committed suicide, I never quoted it as suicide. It was a sudden death. I did that to save the family. Many things that came up that would have been unkind, I softened to meet the occasion.

Maida's motto all of her years was "Give the roses to the living." I asked her to expand on the idea.

> I believe that if we have anything nice to say to make a person feel better or happier, we should give it to the living. Putting wreaths on a tombstone isn't going to do anybody any good. But a nice, kind, encouraging word to the living will. To this day I have people say to me, "I have never forgotten when you said to give the roses to the living, because it is important."
>
> I always think of a beautiful young lady that had the most gorgeous red hair. I met her one day and said, "Oh your hair is just gorgeous." She said, "You know, I was going to stand back, tremble a little bit and not accept the compliment. But I heard you say that when you accept a compliment, you should stand back on your heels, look the person in the eye, and say 'thank you.' So, thank you."

CHIEF EARL OLD PERSON, of Browning, is the lifetime chief of the Blackfeet Tribe. He is a wise, well-spoken man who is revered by his people for the outstanding way he represents them. He appeared several times on the program over the years, promoting North American Indian Days in Browning. One year he brought his costumed dancers with him and encouraged me to wear a buckskin dress and moccasins too, which I did.

As I stood with him asking him to explain the dances we were observing, he suddenly took the microphone from my hand and said, "You do the round dance with them and I will describe what is going on." It was one of those times I had to completely trust a guest. He did such a fine job with the microphone while I danced, that the audience thought it was planned.

Chief Earl Old Person made me an honorary member of the Blackfeet Tribe during the North American Indian Days Celebration in the summer of 1981. I was deeply honored. He gave me the name Kes-Che-Koo-Ma-Kee, which means Princess Thunder Woman, explaining that since I use an unseen power—the airwaves—to communicate with my viewers, it was appropriate that thunder was in my name because thunder is an unseen power to the Blackfeet.

THREE YOUNG MEN FROM MONTANA

Among our early guests on *Today in Montana* was a vocal trio, the Three Young Men from Montana, which included Pat Fox from Hardin; Dick Riddle from Libby; and Bob Ruby from Billings. Dan Snyder and I interviewed them in 1962 and enjoyed hearing about their rapid rise to success.

I had gone to college with them at the University of Montana in Missoula from 1954 to 1957, where they sang together as the Campus Capers. After college, they launched their singing career in New York, at the same time I was living there.

Their big break came when they performed at Julius Monk's Downstairs at the Upstairs in New York in 1961. Their debut drew raves from music reviewers and columnists from the New York press, including *Variety* and the *New Yorker* magazine. Special mention was made of their rendition of "When Johnny Comes Marching Home." They also produced two successful albums of their music—*Folk Song Favorites* and *Fresh New Sounds* from Columbia Records in 1961 and 1962 respectively.

Senator Mike Mansfield praised the trio on the floor of the United States Senate on May 25, 1961, "I wish them every success. Montana is indeed proud of these young musicians from the Treasure State."

Maida was known through her years on the air not only for her kindness and thoughtfulness, but also for her sense of humor on *The Chinook Hour*. I asked her to recall a particularly funny incident.

> I have thousands of them—some of them wouldn't bear repeating. There was a Mr. Aune that was a railroad man in Havre. He didn't like women broadcasters. When he came home for lunch—I was on at two o'clock at that time—his wife had the radio on. He said, "If that's a woman on there, turn her off!" She said that I then came on the air laughing. He was in the next room shaving and be said, "What's that?" She said, "That's that woman from Chinook." He said, "Leave her on, I wanna hear what she's got to say." From then on he was one of my most loyal supporters.

I asked her if she had any inspirations or observations to pass along to young women who are interested in broadcasting.

> I think it's amazing that I could just come right out of the kitchen, wipe the soap suds off my hands and go up and do the program. I didn't have any training. I just always liked to talk. It seems to come naturally. When I was a minister's daughter in Williston, just a little girl, I would often go over and start the morning service when my Dad was delayed and my mother was ill. I'd just tell the folks to turn to hymn number so and so and sing 'til Dad got there.

When I asked her what helped her most, she said it was her early school training.

> We had to learn and memorize many, many things in those days. And, as I have said, "He who never quotes is seldom quoted." I can quote by the yard, because I have read and absorbed things. I think it was my training in school that prepared me for life because I can get up, as my son Clay says, and talk on anything, anytime, anywhere.

Then, knowing she was not the least bit awkward about announcing her age, I asked her to tell the audience what her age was and when her birthday was.

"I think it's amazing that I could just come right out of the kitchen, wipe the soap suds off my hands and go up and do the program. I didn't have any training. I just always liked to talk. It seems to come naturally."

My birthday was November 16, 1895. I had my eightieth birthday party here last Sunday with my family.

We then closed the interview with this KOJM Radio editorial that was written by Stan Stephens, co-owner of KOJM, the day before Maida retired on April 27, 1967. He paid this homage to Maida's more than 5,000 broadcasts on KOJM.

> Broadcasting's greatest legacy is its ability to perform good deeds and genuine public service. It can play the role of a needed communicator and valued servant, or it can be a crass, commercial and often irritating source of noise and trivia. Its course is charted by the people who breathe life into its transmitters, towers, consoles and microphones. It's the quality in people that produces the quality in broadcasting.
>
> Tomorrow KOJM bids farewell to one of its quality people. After an illustrious nineteen years on the airwaves, our remarkable *Chinook Hour* lady Maida McCartney is retiring. In her years on radio, Maida has entertained, informed, consoled, advised and occasionally constructively criticized a vast audience of loyal listeners throughout north Montana.
>
> Many will accept Maida's retirement with disappointment, that the program cannot continue under someone else's supervision. Although no one is indispensable, there are personalities that cannot be duplicated. Maida McCartney is one.
>
> Her broadcast ran the full spectrum of life. She found lost children and pets, chuckled over anecdotes from the *Reader's Digest*, found work for the unemployed, and often a free lunch for the transient. She reported on the accomplishments and tribulations of her "Dear Hearts and Gentle People." Her motto—"Roses to the living"—became a symbolic recognition of the big and little events in the lives of people.

Maida died in 1978 at the age of eighty-two. She gave invaluable service, from letting folks know when a farmer needed help with his harvest, to providing townspeople the latest on that all-important subject: the weather. This type of program connected people inside and outside of that small community of Chinook and made them feel they were not as remote from one another as they might have been. Maida and other pioneer broadcasters may be gone but they will not be forgotten.

"Her broadcast ran the full spectrum of life. She found lost children and pets, chuckled over anecdotes from the Reader's Digest, found work for the unemployed, and often a free lunch for the transient."

Sheila Conners

On July 8, 1987, I interviewed Sheila Conners, who for two years was the director of the Great Falls YWCA and was retiring to become a full-time mother. Prior to her job at the Y, Sheila had been an occupational therapist and she and her husband, attorney Joe Bottomly, had wanted to wait a while before starting their family. She thought changing her career path with the Y position might be less stressful, but she found it just the opposite when her baby arrived. Sheila exemplifies the hard choices that women must make about working and raising a family.

Sheila, who was just stepping down as the YWCA's director, said she had found it more difficult than she had imagined to combine marriage, motherhood and her career. She had had her son six months before our interview.

> I thought I might be able to make this decision during the pregnancy, but when I spoke with other women, they enouraged me to wait to

BOB SCRIVER was a Montana sculptor, who spent his life in his hometown of Browning. As he promoted his major sculptures throughout the years, Bob was a popular guest on *Today in Montana*. He produced a prodigious amount of work that includes the seven and one-half foot tall statue of Charles Russell and the bronze panels depicting Russell's life, located at one of the entrances of the C. M. Russell Museum in Great Falls. He sculpted the Lewis and Clark and Sacagawea statue in Fort Benton's Riverside Park and the Lewis and Clark, York and Seaman statue in Great Falls' Overlook Park. He also produced series on rodeo cowboys, Native Americans and wildlife.

Formerly a music teacher in the Browning school system, he became a self-taught artist and built his Scriver Museum of Montana Wildlife, which was located in Browning for nearly fifty years. A colorful character, he wore a cowboy hat—felt in winter, straw in summer—khaki pants, cowboy boots, a bolo tie and a goatee. He was devoted to animals and always had bobcats and badgers in his studio. He is even known to have carried goose eggs inside his shirt and when they hatched, they would attach themselves to him and follow him everywhere. A determined and jolly man, who preferred to stay where he grew up; he had ranches on the reservation and enjoyed being near his Blackfeet Indian friends.

Bob created a bronze buffalo skull, which he gave to the Great Falls Advertising Federation in 1970 to present to someone who has made a significant contribution to the C. M. Russell Auction or to the field of western art. The buffalo skull was chosen because that was the symbol Russell used to sign his artwork.

Bob died in 1999 at the age of eighty-four. I attended his huge funeral in the Browning High School gym. The high school choir sang and several of the tribe's elders, including Chief Earl Old Person, wearing their colorful headdresses, spoke. Bob was buried in his family plot in the Cut Bank cemetery.

DR. BOB LIND, a human development specialist with the Montana State University's Cooperative Extension Service in Bozeman, was one of my most inspiring guests. Rather stout and jolly, Bob had been a Methodist minister but wanted to do more outreach and help as many people of all ages as he could to give them direction and guidance, so he joined the extension service. He wrote about good parenting, finding happiness in a marriage, understanding aging and understanding adolescence. He saw the humor in life and laughed at so many things. He was a joy to be around.

Bob made frequent appearances on *Today in Montana* and always brought along pieces he had written, which we made available to our viewers.

This is one of his musings, which drew a huge response:

To Wonder Woman and Captain Marvel
(When they know they're not, but think they're supposed to be)

Everybody knows
You can't be all things to all people.
You can't do all things at once.
You can't do all things equally well.
You can't do all things better than everyone else.

Your humanity is showing, just like everyone else's.
So—
You have to find out who you are, and be that.
You have to decide what comes first, and do that.
You have to discover your strengths, and then use them.
You have to learn not to compete with others, because
No one else is in the contest of "being you."

Then you will have learned to accept your own uniqueness.
You will have learned to set priorities and make decisions.
You will have learned to live with your limitations.
You will have learned to give yourself the respect that is due.
And you'll be a most vital mortal.

Dare to believe-
That you are a wonderful, unique person.
That you are a once-in-all-history event.
That it's more than a right, it's your duty to be who you are.
That life is not a problem to solve, but a gift to cherish.
And you'll be able to stay one up on what used to get you down.

make that decision because you just don't know how a child is going to impact your life. A child clearly changes your life, but you don't know how you are going to respond and how you are going to re-prioritize your life.

I put that decision off. I was lucky to have my child nearby in the early months of returning to work. I returned after six weeks and truly felt like physically I wasn't ready. I had my child nearby, though, and that was an opportunity that most women don't have.

She had her child in a day care right at the Y so she could rush out and nurse him. She said that although this was nice, his proximity to her made it difficult because she couldn't keep her full attention on either her job or her baby. "Whatever choice you make, you make a trade off," she said. "I think I thought it was going to be easier than it was. I would be in the middle of an important meeting and they would bring him in and he was ready to eat."

Sheila said that although the staff at the Y was very accommodating—and she didn't feel at all self-conscious about nursing—she said it was still difficult for her to continue working.

Then her son got a little older and was among children, two-year-olds with colds, and he got sick. At one point she set up day care outside the Y and that seemed most appropriate at the time.

After directing the Y for two years, Sheila made the decision to stay home as a full-time mother. I asked her if this was difficult.

I spent a lot of time talking to women before I made my decision to stay home and I am still talking about it. That indicates to me that there are just no clear answers on this. My feeling is that every woman has to figure out in her own mind what she can balance. I think there are women out there who need a career, and that they would not do well staying home full time and would resent the child and that's not in their best interest. And there are women who really struggle with juggling it all.

I think that's the misfortune of our present situation. I think women have a tremendous amount of stress in their lives. Most of them work full-time, raise children, run back and forth to day care centers and then are primarily doing most of the housework.

From the beginning Sheila's husband helped her with the housework and the baby. I asked her to comment on this.

Before our child came we had good delegation of housework and both saw that as a mutual responsibility. When Quinn came along, Joe embraced parenting as well. There is a term—new age father—that I guess applies to him, but I think he really enjoys that participation. I think it's an opportunity to create more balance in men's lives as well.

I pointed out that she was able to make the choice to leave her job and that a lot of women can't make that choice because they needed to make money to help support their family. She, however, had that choice, which was nice.

I feel very grateful for that and I say that a lot. We made some financial sacrifices to make this choice, but there are many families operating in today's society that don't have this choice.

I feel grateful to be able to stay home for a few years and really enjoy this process of watching my child develop. It's a beautiful thing that many women are missing. There is guilt out in the work force about missing that and there are also women home full time who feel guilty that they don't have a job that society perceives as an important position. Women need to support each other no matter what the choice.

I pointed out that she was able to make the choice to leave her job and that a lot of women can't make that choice because they needed to make money to help support their family.

I told Sheila she represented the new woman today in our society who worked quite a while before she had her baby. I imagined even to have a baby was a major decision for her and her husband.

In this day and age, it's another choice to be made. It's not an automatic decision that you will have children. In some ways I think that's good because it's a very important decision to make. It should be a tough decision because it's a big responsibility. My husband and I have taken time to develop our marriage and get that stability there before we decided to have a child.

On the other hand I spoke with a woman recently who had her children very early and was at home. Now she went back to school and is developing her career. She was saying, "I didn't get to do this earlier on and now I'm doing it."

Life has its cycles. I'm glad about the choices I have made.

Today Sheila is the mother of two teenage boys and she and her husband Joe live with their boys in Kalispell. Along with raising her active family, she works as an occupational therapist assists her husband in his law offices and does volunteer work.

Guests With Snakes

Of the all the guests I interviewed, the most memorable have been guests with snakes. There are two types of people. Those who aren't afraid of snakes at all. And those, like me, who are deathly afraid of them.

One of my easiest snake-related interviews with Hank Lentfer of Livingston. We visited him at his home and he showed us a huge barrel in his backyard filled with live snakes, the sight of which sent a shiver down my spine.

Hank had a hobby making jewelry from the vertebrae of their spinal columns and I invited him to bring some of his snake jewelry on the show. He also brought a live bull snake to show, which was unnerving for me. I still have one of Hank's snake vertebrae necklaces, which I often wear.

To promote the Circus Vargas when it came to town in 1981, Oz the Clown appeared on the show with his pet boa constrictor, George. As we were wrapping up the interview, Oz suddenly draped the snake around my shoulders.

"He doesn't kiss on the first date," Oz said.

Of the all the guests I interviewed, the most memorable have been guests with snakes. There are two types of people. Those who aren't afraid of snakes at all. And those, like me, who are deathly afraid of them.

I was panic-stricken. I stood there, frozen, as he gave his pitch about coming to the circus. When he was finished, I couldn't ask him fast enough to take George off my shoulders. When he did, I breathed a sigh of relief.

I told him the snake felt ice cold. Oz denied it. George didn't say a word!

Janice Ypma of Manhattan, the self-proclaimed "snake lady" of Montana, asked if she could show her three pet snakes on our program. I agreed to tape an interview with her. She arrived with the snakes in three gunny sacks. She took out the first two as she talked about their characteristics—first a black snake and then a boa constrictor. She put them carefully back in their sacks. Then she pulled the third snake out of its sack. It was a twelve-foot python. She stood up so the snake could crawl all the way up her body and come down the other side. I was aghast. I could hardly ask intelligent questions as she finished describing the characteristics of the snake.

At the end of the interview, the production crew (who knew about my fear of snakes) let the tape continue to run. Janice briefly took her eyes off the python to reach for its gunny sack and it immediately slithered up on the couch where I was sitting. I looked at the TV monitor and saw this woman sitting on the couch with a twelve-foot python coming right at her. When I realized it was me, I screamed, and pulled my feet up under me. Janice reacted quickly, grabbed her pet and stuffed it back in the gunny sack. The station used this footage to promote the show, with a voice-over saying, "Don't miss *Today in Montana*, anything can happen." They ran this promotional ad until viewers asked that it be taken off the air because it was too scary. I felt vindicated.

But the most frightening snake incident and my most memorable guest was with a rancher from Raynesford, Cyril Colarchek.

TOP: Hank Lentfer of Livingston displaying the jewelry he made from snake vertebrae.

BOTTOM: Cyril Colarchek's live rattlesnake displayed on a buffalo skull.

He told me he was a rattlesnake handler and would enjoy showing his skills on our program. Having spent the first five years of my life in rattlesnake country on a ranch near Winston, I have an innate fear of rattlesnakes

When I interviewed him in 1967, sure enough he brought a live rattlesnake into the studio and laid it on the floor. He made it strike by teasing it with a rubber ball at the end of a stick. Then he grabbed it behind the head, picked it up and showed its fangs to the camera. The camera girl, Susie Rothenbuehler, was trying to do her job the best she could looking down the mouth of a rattler.

He then put it back down on the floor, stepped on its head, took a knife and slit it up the belly. Thirteen baby rattlers spilled out onto the floor. Someone in the studio had the sense to grab a shovel, scoop up the baby rattlers, take them outside and bury them in the ground, knowing that they were poisonous too. In the meantime, Cyril skinned the rattler (he later gave the skin to Susie, who made it into a hatband) and cut off the rattle. He placed the rattle in my hand. It was still moving.

I can't remember one thing I said in that interview. I do remember that Cyril's wife, who had accompanied him, said she would divorce him if he ever did anything like that again.

The reaction to Cyril was the most dramatic we ever received. It ranged from one viewer who said, "I'm going to report you to the Association for the Prevention of Cruelty to Animals," to another viewer who said, "That was the best show you have ever done. Why don't you dress out a deer sometime?"

Cyril Colarchek of Raynesford who brought a live rattlesnake on the show in 1967 and slaughtered it on the air. Thirteen baby rattlers spilled out on to the studio floor.

—4—
On Location

Almost from the beginning of my career at KRTV, we did interviews on location. Our mobile equipment enabled us to go to the scene and meet people, see places and cover events right where they were happening. This capability expanded our audience and also helped us get to know the people personally who were our viewers. The risk of on-location interviews was that equipment could fail and if you didn't have some kind of backup, you were in trouble. That happened once to me in Browning when I was fortunate to have two cameramen with me. The footage one of them took turned out. The footage of the second cameraman didn't. Without that back-up, that trip would have been wasted. Then, of course, there is always the challenge of weather in Montana. But more often than not, it seemed that through rain, snow or sleet, we were able to get the story.

The cameramen and women who worked on these on-location interviews were a very special group of my co-workers. As we traveled miles to put these shows together, from towns as far-flung as Glendive to West Yellowstone, we shared the rigors of traveling, as well as innumerable cups of coffee. They included Wayne Schultz, John Hildenstab, Carl Kochman, Lynn Fleming, Joe Lawson, Tim Luinstra, Lindsay McNay, Joe Stark, Ian Marquand, Carey Olson, Bill Leach and Jim Turner.

State Fairs

Covering the Montana State Fair from 1962 to 1988 was fun and challenging, especially in the early years when all other programming on KRTV was pre-empted for our live reports from the state fairgrounds.

During those early years, we were on the fairgrounds with our mobile unit from 8 a.m. until 6 p.m. Besides interviewing the stars

---

During those early years, we were on the fairgrounds with our mobile unit from 8 a.m. until 6 p.m. Besides interviewing the stars of the night show, we talked to every blue-ribbon winner of every exhibit we could find, from photographers to artists, from ranch wives to merchants.

of the night show, we talked to every blue-ribbon winner of every exhibit we could find, from photographers to artists, from ranch wives to merchants. We also covered the horse races. We featured winners of the Montana Cowbelles–sponsored beef cook-off, prize-winning animals, 4-H kids, hobbyists, homemakers, flower arrangers, fair executives, and the workers from some of the fair's most popular food booths. I had fun competing in the Media Cow Milking Contest and the Cowchip Throwing. One year our set was outdoors without any shelter or shade and I got a severe case of sun poisoning. I became very ill and between interviews I had to run to the bathroom, which made it tricky indeed to get through the day!

Dan Snyder and I often interviewed our guests together. One celebrity we talked to was Jimmy Dean, a country singer and later founder of his own sausage company. He was open and friendly and even attended a Great Falls Press Club party while he was in town. Other celebrities we interviewed on location included singer Dennis Day and comedian George Gobel. They were both delightful, laughing and cracking jokes with us. One of the most difficult interviews I did there was with World-Champion Cowboy Benny Reynolds, the pride of Melrose. This handsome and talented cowboy who had made such a name for himself on the rodeo circuit was extremely short on words. The harder I tried to come up with questions that would inspire wordier answers, the more recalcitrant he became. As a matter of fact, he used only two words to answer most of my questions, "Yep" and "Nope."

Gentle Ben and his trainers with Norma at the State Fair in 1969.

Eight Surrounding Communities

Among my most memorable on-location interviews were those salutes that were filmed in the eight communities surrounding Great Falls: Augusta, Belt, Cascade, Choteau, Conrad, Fort Benton, Shelby and Valier. With so much attention given to cities, we decided it was time to spotlight small towns. During 1965 and 1966, we took our mobile videotape equipment and film camera to these neighboring towns all with populations under 5,000.

I produced the series and did the interviews. Our crew consisted of Dan Snyder, technical director and interviewer; Wayne Schultz and John Hildenstab, cameramen; and Jess Waymire, chief engineer. The series was met with enthusiasm and the response from our viewers was gratifying.

The key to our success was that we would find a host in each community who lined us up with interesting people and made sure we presented their town in the best possible way. The hosts were all long-time residents of their town, "movers and shakers," and they were knowledgeable about its history. Our hosts were Art Nett from Augusta, Joe Morris from Belt, Stu Moore from Cascade, Olga Monkman from Choteau, Dorothy Floerchinger from Conrad,

Hosts of salutes to the eight north central Montana communities in 1966 with Norma and Dan Snyder. First row, from left: Olga Monkman, Choteau; Dorothy Floerchinger, Conrad; Veta Marsh, Valier; Theo Bartschi, Shelby. Second row, from left: Stu Moore, Cascade; Joe Morris, Belt; Art Nett, Augusta; Grover Schmidt, Fort Benton. BILL SHACKLEFORD

Grover Schmidt from Fort Benton, Theo Bartschi from Shelby, and Veta Marsh from Valier.

We taped a week's worth of programs in one day in each town. We interviewed a wide spectrum of people from mayors to businessmen, from artists to educators, from old–timers to librarians. These guests were ordinary people doing extraordinary things. They were neighbors and friends in their community and their fellow townspeople enjoyed seeing them on television. In addition, businesses in the communities bought advertising for the shows that ran during the salutes and they reported a noticeable increase in sales.

Following the series, all of the hosts appeared on *Today in Montana* and received certificates of appreciation for their cooperation. At a luncheon after the series, the hosts and their spouses received gifts from Great Falls businesses.

The Queen's Visit

In 1973 KRTV cameraman Carl Kochman and I traveled six hours north to Canada to cover Queen Elizabeth II's visit to Calgary. She was there for the centennial of the Royal Canadian Mounted Police.

When Queen Elizabeth II made her appearance, at the Calgary airport, escorted by her husband Prince Philip, there was a crush of media, reporters bearing microphones, cameras and cameramen that we had not anticipated. As the photographers jostled for the best position, Carl nearly got trampled to death. Fortunately he did get some useable footage and so did I with my still camera.

I was struck by how petite the Queen was and by her beautiful skin. Wearing a floral dress and hat, she smiled and waved. The Prince was tall and handsome and walked respectfully behind her.

To get a bird's-eye view of the Royal Canadian Mounted Police musical ride—or Musical Mounties—Carl and I climbed up a ladder to the top of a building to get shots of the Mounties in their red coats and flat-brimmed brown Stetsons riding in formation on their beautiful black horses on the parade grounds below. This was a tough job as Carl had to haul the heavy camera equipment with him and this was scary for me as I dislike heights. Nonetheless, it was an ideal perch to watch the thirty-two riders and their horses perform intricate cavalry drills to music. We got great footage as the Mounties and their mounts pranced around the parade grounds.

Later, I interviewed several officials with the Royal Canadian Mounted Police and found them cooperative and impressive. They

We interviewed a wide spectrum of people from mayors to businessmen, from artists to educators, from old–timers to librarians. These guests were ordinary people doing extraordinary things. They were neighbors and friends in their community and their fellow townspeople enjoyed seeing them on television.

told me about the important role the Mounties have played during their 100 years of service as law enforcement officers in Canada and how meaningful it was for them to have Queen Elizabeth II and Prince Philip there for their centennial.

Broadwater Hotel Auction

The Broadwater Hotel and Natatorium was the brightest jewel in a string of accomplishments of Colonel Charles A. Broadwater, a Helena businessman. Opened in 1889 on Helena's western edge, it was set on lavishly landscaped grounds. The hotel, surrounded by broad verandas, was finished in the great Victorian tradition of antique oak, velvet carpets, stained-glass windows and cut-crystal decorations. The Natatorium, built along Moorish lines, was 300 feet long and 100 feet wide, and its precise temperature was maintained by hot and cold water that issued from a fountain of boulders at one end.

After four decades of service, the natatorium was badly damaged during the earthquakes in 1935 and torn down. The hotel also suffered severe damage and for many years stood boarded up as a reminder of Helena's elegant past, when the town had, reputedly, more millionaires per capita than anywhere else in the United States.

I interviewed Marion Broadwater Kuhr of Havre, whose father was a first cousin of Charles Broadwater. Marion said she had stayed at the Broadwater Hotel when she was a child. She remembered the linen tablecloths and fine china in the dining room and the linen sheets and linen pillowcases on the beds. She enjoyed climbing the steps up the cupola on the roof.

In 1974 an auction was held to dispose of all the remaining pieces of the building—everything was sold from the beautiful stained glass windows, doors, marble bathtubs and sinks down to the light fixtures. I was able to buy two keepsakes at the auction. One was a hammered brass doorknob which we put on a closet door in our home and the other was a white marble pedestal from one of the bathtubs, which serves as a candle stand.

Following the auction, the hotel was torn down. All that remains of the original structure is one of the cupolas that now stands in a park on the east side of Helena. Fortunately there are photographs of the Broadwater, which show the structures in all their magnificence when they were proclaimed, "the place to effectually and completely recover lost nerve force and to rebuild a debilitated system."

The Broadwater Hotel and Natatorium was the brightest jewel in a string of accomplishments of Colonel Charles A. Broadwater, a Helena businessman. Opened in 1889 on Helena's western edge, it was set on lavishly landscaped grounds.

The Miles City Bucking Horse Sale

In 1978 cameraman Carl Kochman and I had a grand experience covering the Bucking Horse Sale in Miles City. Designated world-famous because it is the oldest sale of its kind, dating back to 1951, ranchers provide the horses they were unable to break and rodeo producers come to buy them. Descent, named Bucking Horse of the Year, was one of the great bucking horses that came out of the sale.

Miles City, a town of 10,000, doubles in size during the sale held the third weekend in May. Prior to the sale, townspeople and visitors enjoy a parade of horses, floats, marching units and antique cars.

At the sale, Carl insisted on positioning himself in front of the chutes. As the horses came out of the chutes, twisting and turning, some nearly climbing right over the chute itself, I feared more than once that we would be run over. Nevertheless, Carl managed to jump to safety and got close-up shots of the bucking horses and their riders struggling to stay on or falling heavily to the ground. Just once did he get jostled by a pickup rider.

I had a memorable interview with Cy Taillon, the dean of rodeo announcers, who helped found the sale and was its announcer for many years. He was one of the original Cowboy Turtles, who started the first professional rodeo organization at Boston Gardens in 1936. They got their name because they were slow, like turtles, to get organized. The Cowboys Turtle Association was the forerunner of the Rodeo Cowboys Association, which has become the Professional Rodeo Cowboys Association. The PRCA's bylaws were written by Cy. He had one of the best voices I had heard on a microphone: as each rider came out he would call, encourage and extol the attributes of the rider as well as provide a vivid description of the horse in his deep, velvety voice. He was the first rodeo announcer to make a lifetime career of handling the microphone for the sport of cowboys and cowgirls. He obviously loved what he did.

He died in Great Falls in 1980 at the age of seventy-two. The Miles City Bucking Horse Sale is dedicated to Cy and also to Boyd Hirsh, a longtime supporter of the sale.

On Sunday morning, following the sale, Carl and I received permission from owners to do a piece on the historic back bars of Miles City, several of which are nearly a century old. We visited the Bison, the Montana, the Range Riders and Trail's End. Some of them had come up the Yellowstone River. They were old, hand-carved, with big mirrors and booths and a lot of living had gone on inside them. The mirror at the Montana Bar had a bullet hole in it.

At the sale, Carl insisted on positioning himself in front of the chutes. As the horses came out of the chutes, twisting and turning, some nearly climbing right over the chute itself, I feared more than once that we would be run over.

Evel Knievel

One of Montana's most famous citizens is Evel Knievel, motorcycle daredevil who, in the course of his career starting in 1965, made 300 jumps and broke 35 bones. In 1974 he arranged his most famous stunt, an attempted jump over Idaho's Snake River Canyon in a rocket-powered motorcycle. The attempt failed when the craft's parachute opened prematurely but Evel survived. Among his famous quotes are: "I've always lived by the creed that you're never a failure in life when you fall, as long as you try and get up." His other was: "Life is an everyday battle at keeping death at a comfortable distance."

I did a series of interviews with Evel in 1979 in his hometown of Butte. I first talked to him about his art work in his studio near his large ranch style home situated near the Butte golf course. I was surprised to learn painting was a favorite hobby of his. He was happy to show his work to me. His favorite subjects were western scenes and wildlife, which he sold in limited edition prints in art galleries nationwide. He next took me for a ride in his custom-made golf cart, saying golf was a favorite sport of his.

Finally, he showed me his diamond rings. He invested in diamonds as a kind of insurance—as a daredevil he couldn't get regular life insurance. One of his rings was in the shape of a motorcycle and was valued at $100,000.

George Hamilton portrayed Evel in the 1971 movie *Evel Knievel*. George Eads played him in the 2004 TV movie *Evel Knievel*. His son Robbie Knievel is following in his father's footsteps as a daredevil motorcycle jumper. Butte now holds Evel Knievel Days the last weekend in July, which attracts motorcyclists from around the country.

Evel Knievel with Norma in Butte in 1979.

Evel's motorcycle and memorabilia are displayed by the Smithsonian Institute in their Museum of American History in Washington, D. C., where he is presented as America's legendary daredevil.

The Parrot

In 1982 I interviewed Nancy Duensing and her sons, David and Dusty Duensing, who owned the Parrot Confectionary in Helena. I also interviewed the original owner, Mrs. W. R. "Postie" Post. The Parrot, which has been on Last Chance Gulch since April 28, 1922, claims to be Helena's oldest downtown business. Generations of high school sweethearts, children, politicians and businesspeople have stood in front of the glass cases to order hand-dipped chocolates or homemade caramels or have cozied together in one of the twelve booths to order sundaes made with homemade ice cream and toppings. They feature two menu items: turkey tamales and chili.

My favorite part of the interview was visiting the dipping room where the confectioners hand-dip the chocolates. The Duensing brothers pour six tons of sugar and three tons of chocolate into their copper kettles every year and turn it into fancy candies. I topped off my visit with two of my favorites: a caramel nut parfait and the Parrot's namesake candy of caramel, nuts and chocolate.

Norma with Nancy Duensing, co-owner of Helena's The Parrot and Ianthe "Postie" Post, the original owner, in April 1982.

Little has changed about the decor of the Parrot since the 1950s, when it was a favorite hang-out of mine in high school. The glass display cases, the candy, the soda fountain, the booths, the huge collection of elephants in ceramic, wood, plastic and china vie for space with the ceramic parrots that are all still there. It has never been franchised. It is a one-of-a-kind, home-owned business. People who leave Helena and return years later or even decades

110

later are always relieved and grateful that the Parrot has not changed.

During holidays, the Parrot ships boxes of candy all over the world—to Africa, Australia, Europe, Japan and to South America. One Helena native, the late Bill Roth, U.S. Senator from Delaware, would order Parrot candy for his staff at Christmastime. The Parrot's slogan is: "It talks for itself." Thousands of satisfied customers over the years agree. I always stop by when I am in Helena.

Montana's Island Home: ANUKA of Salmon Lake

In 1987, I interviewed Dr. Bruce Vorhauer—the biomedical engineer who invented the contraceptive sponge—at Anuka, his 12,000 square foot, fifty-five room corporate retreat on Sourdough Island in the middle of Salmon Lake. Bruce had spared no expense in building his home. My cameramen Joe Lawson and Tim Luinstra and I were the first media group to be permitted inside the home.

The living room featured massive leather sofas around a sunken conversation pit, a giant stone fireplace, a twenty-seven foot bookcase, giant-screen television and wet bar. The room's colors were blue and tan for the sky and earth. There were ten bedrooms in his home, fourteen bathrooms, three kitchens, gymnasium, a Jacuzzi, game room, five fireplaces, fifty telephones, twenty television sets, five computer lines, a satellite dish and five heating and cooling systems. And there was an extensive western art collection by such artists as Chester Fields, Joe Halko and Jim Pasma. Six hand-carved solid oak doors were done by Don Lincoln and there were 200 cedar lighting fixtures.

Bruce said he named the home Anuka after a shortened Blackfeet word that means "today." This was appropriate since the brand name for his sponge was "Today." (In 1986, it was the largest over-the-counter product of its kind with sales of $65,000,000 in thirteen countries). He said Today helped him pay for the home and he also said, "We live in today. Tomorrow will come and yesterday is gone. I thought it was significant to call it Anuka."

When I talked with Bruce about his home, he said that when he first built it people were quite skeptical because "it looked like a mining camp there." But in the end, he said, "We protected the environment. We only took out two trees. The main criticism came from someone who didn't live here."

When I asked him about the price of the home, which was

The Duensing brothers pour six tons of sugar and three tons of chocolate into their copper kettles every year and turn it into fancy candies. I topped off my visit with two of my favorites: a caramel nut parfait and the Parrot's namesake candy of caramel, nuts and chocolate.

$7,500,000, Bruce said, "I didn't operate on a budget. I started on an unlimited budget and managed to exceed it. There is a lot of pride in the workmanship and you can see it throughout the house. Nothing here is done halfway."

Bruce was planning to marry his fiancée, Sara, in the house, but when she died, he lost interest in it and put it on the market. When I asked him about selling it, he said that he didn't think he would sell it, that there was a good chance he would use it in a new business he might be starting. He said he would eventually like to transfer the house to the University of Montana as an international conference center to show the world, "we don't live in log cabins in Montana."

Two things make this interview poignant to me. Bruce died in 1992 at the age of fifty and eventually his home was donated to the University of Montana, where it is now maintained as a conference site. Secondly, it was the forerunner for the many homes that have been built since then by the very wealthy who have continued to discover that Montana is a very special place to live.

Jerome Hayes

In 1972 I was at the old Montana State Prison in Deer Lodge. What could have been a very dangerous experience turned out to be a memorable one when I was allowed into solitary confinement (called the "hole") to interview inmate Jerome Hayes. The small cell was dark and dingy, its only furnishings a mattress and a bucket on the floor. Jerome had been put there for bad behavior.

The guard stood outside the open door as I talked to him just inside the door. Looking back I realized what a risk that might have been but I needn't have worried. Although he was a tall, gaunt man, grateful for any outside attention, he was so demoralized when I met him he seemed to me more like a little boy. I don't remember much of what we visited about—only the dark cell in which we talked. Later, however, Jerome corresponded with me after my visit. He even sent me a cross and a pair of praying hands earrings he had made in prison. He died of cancer not too long after our meeting.

Jeannette Rankin Statue Dedication

On May 30, 1985, I covered the dedication of the Jeannette Rankin statue in Statuary Hall in the Capitol Building in Washington, D.C. The statue of Montana's famed stateswoman was created by Great Falls' sculptor Terry Mimnaugh. Rankin's statue joined cowboy artist Charles Russell's statue, which was created by John Weaver.

What could have been a very dangerous experience turned out to be a memorable one when I was allowed into solitary confinement (called the "hole") to interview Jerome Hayes. The small cell was dark and dingy, its only furnishings a mattress and a bucket on the floor.

Each state is permitted to have two statues in the Capitol.

The oldest of eleven children, Rankin graduated from Montana State University in Missoula in 1902. In 1910, she was the first woman to speak to the Montana Legislature. A suffragist and lifelong pacifist, in 1914 Jeannette led a successful drive for women's voting rights in her native state of Montana. When she was elected to the United States Congress in 1916, Jeannette was not only the first woman to be elected to Congress, she was the first woman in the world to be elected to a parliamentary body. She voted against America's entry into WWI and again when she served a second term in Congress against entry into WWII.

Dedication ceremony of Jeannette Rankin Statue in the U.S. Capitol on May 1, 1985. From left: Senator Max Baucus, Governor Ted Schwinden, sculptor Terry Mimnaugh, House Speaker Senator Thomas "Tip" O'Neill, Congressman Ron Marlenee, Rankin nephew Tom Kinney, Senator John Melcher and Congressman Pat Williams.

The entire Montana delegation and other dignitaries spoke at the dedication.

Congressman Pat Williams described her as "grace under pressure." Congressman Ron Marlenee, who said while he didn't agree with everything she stood for, he described her as "determined, controversial and very commited to her beliefs."

Senator Max Baucus said that when he heard her speak at the Montana Constitutional Convention in 1972, he saw "a gutsy, tough, courageous, inspiring, wonderful person. I thought to myself, my gosh, why isn't Jeannette a member of the Montana Constitutional Convention?"

Historian Joan Hoff-Wilson said that on top of her willingness to assume office, one of the unique and controversial features of Jeannette's views was that "long before public opinion polls told us that women in the United States tended to favor peaceful solutions to problems more than men, Jeannette had come to a singular conclusion that women and peace were inseparable."

Governor Ted Schwinden dedicated the statue to the national's capitol and honored her for her "unswerving commitment to democracy..."to the ideal that each person should be free in her own words to serve humanity as a separate and distinct individuality. Whether her causes were in or out of fashion, Jeannette pursued them with uncommon integrity, with keen intelligence, and with unflagging dedication."

House Speaker Thomas "Tip" O'Neill accepted the statue on behalf of the House of Representatives, with the comment that "Jeannette Rankin opened the doors of political opportunity for all American women."

Following the dedication, I asked Frances Elge, who had been Jeannette Rankin's administrative assistant, about how she thought Jeannette would have reacted to the ceremony:

> I think she would have been delighted with the speeches and the reiteration and reinforcement of other strong positions against war.

When I asked Terry Mimnaugh, who was only thirty years old at the time, about her reaction to the ceremony, she laughed. "Remember when we had our last interview, I told you that I was going to need a control tower to land all the butterflies? Today they are so big, they have landing lights."

The statue of Jeannette Rankin now stands with ninety-three other Americans in Statuary Hall. The engraving on the statue of Jeannette Rankin, 1880-1973, reads: "I cannot vote for war" and is a permanent reminder of this woman's lifetime dedication to the cause of peace. A duplicate statue is in the Montana State Capitol in Helena.

Jeannette died in 1973, one month away from her ninety-third birthday.

Gilcrease Museum

In 1987, I covered the dedication of the expanded Gilcrease Museum in Tulsa, Oklahoma, with the help of a cameraman from one of the local television stations. The Gilcrease has the largest collection of western art, artifacts and documents about the development of the Americas. The $12 million dollar expansion of the original museum created in 1949 tripled the number of galleries and storage areas, but even then only fifteen percent of the collection could be shown at one time. Coming from Great Falls to the Gilcrease Museum in Tulsa—which I thought of as the Louvre of western art—made me appreciate Charles Russell even more because of the number and quality of original Russells in its collection.

When I asked Fred Myers, the museum director, to talk about

The statue of Jeannette Rankin now stands with ninety-three other Americans in Statuary Hall.

the museum's namesake, he described Thomas Gilcrease as a very quiet man. "He was an oil man, who had an Indian background," he said. "Without telling anybody he was doing it, he simply went out and put together the best western art collection anywhere."

Fred said the collection included more than 10,000 artworks, 50,000 artifacts, and 90,000 documents and books. He added that Thomas Gilcrease also had the added advantage of acquiring the material in the 1940s and early '50s. "This material was out there," he said, "and few other people were paying attention to it, so the material was relatively inexpensively priced."

The museum has one of the world's greatest collections of Russells. They own eighty-eight Russell works and some of the most well-known Russell paintings. These include *Jerked Down*, which was selected for use on a U.S. postage stamp in 1964, *Meat's Not Meat Until It's In the Pan*, showing a hunter who has just shot a big horn sheep high on the side of a mountain in a nearly impossible place to retrieve it that brings a smile to everyone's lips and *Her Heart is On the Ground*, showing an Indian woman grieving for the loss of her husband, one of the most poignant paintings Russell ever painted.

The museum features works by over 300 other artists. It contains the world's largest collection of paintings by O.C. Seltzer, more than 400, and paintings and fifty-five bronzes by Frederic Remington, including one of his most famous bronzes, *Coming Through the Rye.*

The building was funded, Fred said, by a combination of public and private money. Nearly $6 million was raised by the Gilcrease Museum Association fund drive that concentrated on people who could contribute more than $25,000. Myers said the fund drive, which took place during the oil boom, took only two months.

The reception and dinner for the grand opening gala was an elegant affair. The menu was illustrated with a pen and ink drawing on a reproduction of the personal letterhead of Charles Russell from the Gilcrease collection. It featured Shoshone Falls Salmon and Peeled Cucumber with Caviar, Beef Remington with Berninghaus Sauce, Pheasant Audubon, Squash Blossoms, Native American Vegetables, Corn Maiden Muffins, Black Hawk Bavarian Pie with Whirling Thunder Sauce, Choice of Red and White Seltzers and Pre-Columbian Coffee.

North American Indian Days in Browning

This annual celebration and powwow, which has been running since 1952, attracts some of the best American Indian dancers, singers and drummers from throughout Montana, the United States

> *The museum has one of the world's greatest collections of Russells. They own eighty-eight Russell works and some of the most well-known Russell paintings.*

Norma's induction ceremony into the Blackfeet Tribe at North American Indian Days in Browning, Montana, July 10, 1981. Blackfeet council members, from left: George Old Person, Sam Young Running Crane, John de Rouche and Chief Earl Old Person, who conducted the ceremony and gave Norma her Blackfeet name: *Kes-Che-Koo-Ma-Kee* or Princess Thunder Woman.

and Canada. My cameraman Joe Lawson and I made arrangements with Chief Earl Old Person in 1987 to get good footage and talk to key participants in the celebration. In addition to the Chief, who explained the importance of the gathering as the some of the traditions of the Indian people, I talked to some of the dancers, the drummers and organizers. Joe captured the different dance competitions—the jingle dance, the fancy dance and the chicken dance which highlighted the dancers' skills and the spectacular costumes. His footage of the competing drum groups with their steady, thunder-like beat and haunting songs was equally impressive. The tipis with their colorful symbols and the mountains of Glacier Park, made for an awesome backdrop for this spectacle.

The Chief had said he would arrange a place for us to stay. When we arrived, the Chief announced that we could share a tipi with him and his family. As much fun as that might have been, we declined. We needed to get some rest and be fresh for our next full day of filming.

There was one problem. There were no spare rooms in the motels in Browning.

I asked the mayor if he could help us and he said his daughter owned one of the motels. When she learned of our plight, she and her husband moved out of their room and gave it to us for the night.

It had two double beds. Joe used the bathroom first, jumped into one of the beds and pulled the covers over his head. I did the same in the other bed.

To this day, Joe and I laugh about the night we shared a motel room in Browning!

My most recent attendance at North American Indian Days was on July 10, 2004. Chief Earl Old Person had invited me to be a part of the honoring ceremony for his late wife Doris, a long-time educator. Wearing my Indian costume, I gathered with his family in the center of the parade grounds as someone read about Doris's accomplishments. My thirteen- year- old grandson, Jack Schrader, was with me, and the two of us moved slowly with Doris' family around the grounds as members of the audience one at a time stepped forward and took our hands. No words were spoken, but in the hand clasp I felt the sympathy they expressed about her passing. Finally the family did a give-away, presenting dozens of gifts to those gathered for the ceremony. When Twila Day Child, Earl's granddaughter, stepped forward and placed a star quilt around my shoulders as my gift, I felt the tears well up in my eyes. I had known Twila since she first danced at the Russell Auction when she was three years old. She is now a wife and mother of her own three-year-old daughter. The quilt is displayed on our bed, a reminder of a special friendship I have had through the years with Earl and Doris.

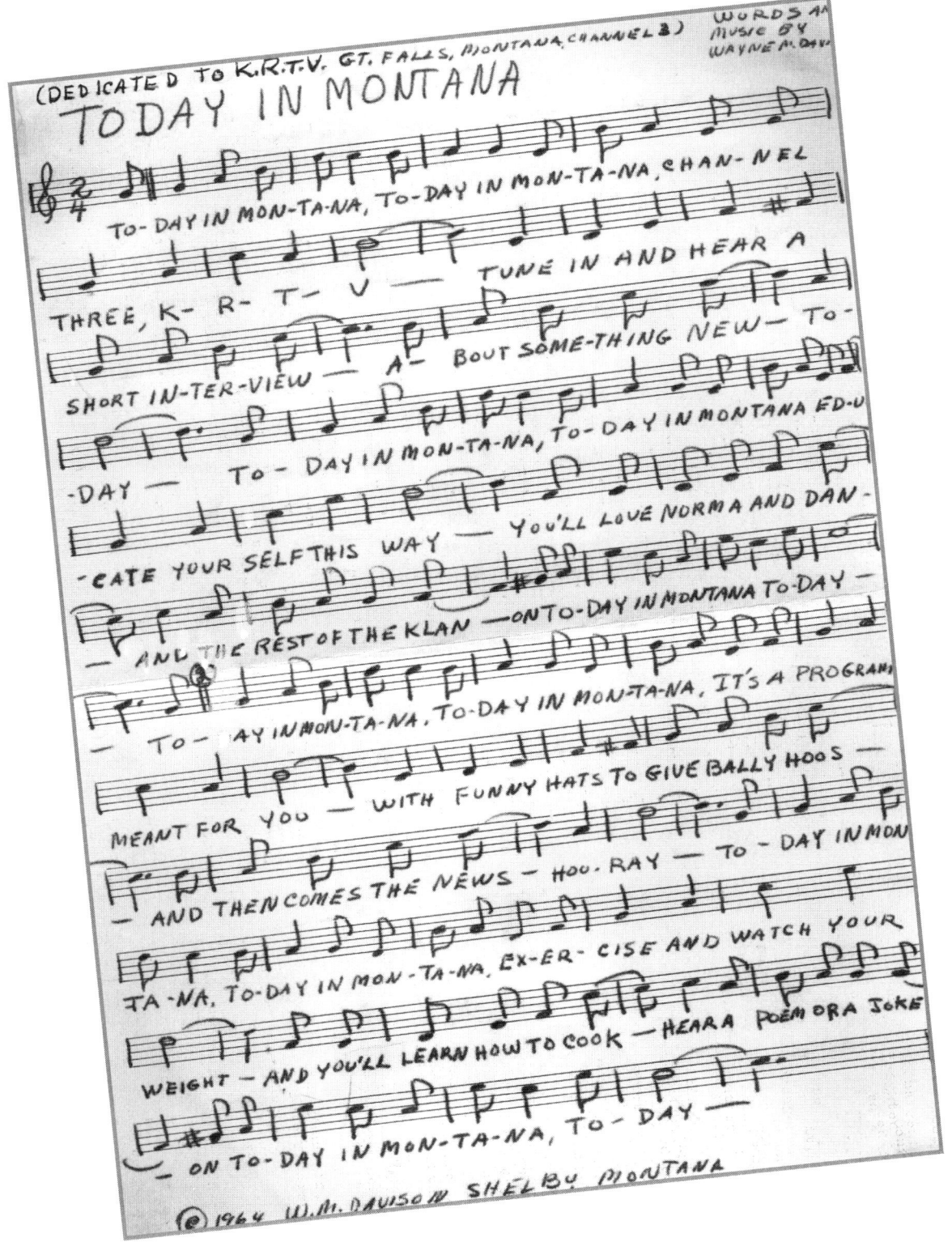

An original song written for *Today in Montana*, by Wayne Davison of Shelby, in 1964.

—5—
Off Camera

President John F. Kennedy in the Electric City

President John F. Kennedy visited Great Falls on September 26, 1963. It was an unforgettable day. Nearly 100,000 people saw the President as his motorcade took him from the Great Falls International Airport to the Great Falls High School's Memorial Stadium, where he was scheduled to speak. Throngs of people lined the streets, waving as his motorcade drove past. People stood on rooftops. There were even people perched in the trees that lined the streets.

I had a reserved seat right down in front of his podium and a press pass that entitled me to get a closer view of the President than I expected. I had my tape recorder with me to tape portions of his speech for *Today in Montana*.

Here are the closing words of his speech, which I captured on audiotape:

> This sun and this sky, which shines over Montana, can be, I believe, the kind of inspiration to us all to recognize what a great single country we have. Fifty separate states but one people, living here in the United States, building this country and maintaining the watch around the globe. This is the opportunity before us, as well as the responsibility.

Following his remarks he walked into the press area—just a roped off section of the stadium. Just as he walked up to me, two photographers snapped pictures of me standing next to him. I have copies of them both. It was a thrilling moment. I had worn a red wig and an aqua dress and was beaming from ear to ear.

President Kennedy then shook hands with people in the crowd. He shook hands with ninety-five-year-old John Kimmel, an early-day

---

The President came to our town yesterday

It was a memorable experience in every way.

The sky was clear as the big jet set down

And as the President appeared he heard the crowd's cheers resound.

RESERVED SEAT
for address of
JOHN F. KENNEDY
PRESIDENT OF THE UNITED STATES

September 26, 1963
Memorial Stadium, Great Falls High School
GREAT FALLS, MONTANA

Your seat will be held until 12:15 P.M. only

Norma with President John F. Kennedy at the Great Falls Memorial Stadium on September 26, 1963. People also pictured are, from left: Undersheriff Bob Hunter; John Kimmell, 95, an early day law enforcement officer; and Donna Carrico, 13, daughter of Fire Chief Charles Carrico.

law enforcement officer in Great Falls. In the photograph, the President was closely surrounded by others, including Under Sheriff Bob Hunter and Donna Carrico, the thirteen-year-old daughter of Fire Chief Charles Carrico.

Following the President's visit, I wrote this poem:

The President Came to Our Town Yesterday

The President came to our town yesterday
It was a memorable experience in every way.
The sky was clear as the big jet set down
And as the President appeared he heard
the crowd's cheers resound.
Memorial Stadium was filled to the brim

As people came from far and near
For a look at him.
His words rang out loud and clear
As he spoke of our country
and the things we hold dear.
Peace, liberty, freedom we must uphold he cried
So generations to come can say that we tried
To keep our country the strongest nation on earth
To fulfill our dreams so constant from birth.
Children tugged at their parents
Old folks nodded in the hot sun
But when his speech ended
We knew we had won.
A chance for a while to share in a tradition
Of hearing our President speak
Of our country's great mission.
And for years to come
We would remember that bright autumn day
When the President came to our town
And had these words to say:
"This day has been a memorable one for me."
And it was for young and old Montanans
And also for me.

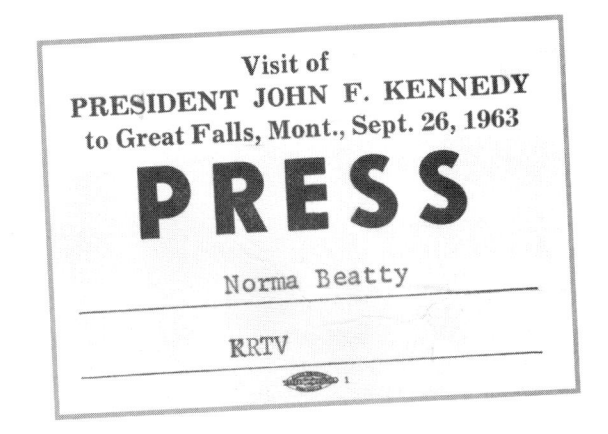

I sent a copy of the poem to the President soon afterward, and on October 4, 1963, I received this reply from the President's press secretary, Pierre Salinger:

Dear Miss Beatty:
The President was very touched by your letter and more especially by your poem. He has asked me to send you his sincere thanks and best wishes.
I would like to add my thanks.

I was in the control room at KRTV on November 22, 1963, when the news came over the wire that President Kennedy had been assassinated in Dallas, Texas. It was one of the greatest tragedies in our nation's history.

Governor Ronald Reagan

In 1967, I met Ronald Reagan when he was governor of California. He was at the Rainbow Hotel in Great Falls for a recep-

Norma with California Governor Ronald Reagan, and Montana Governor Tim Babcock at a reception at the Rainbow Hotel in Great Falls in 1967.

tion with Montana Governor Tim Babcock. The three of us had a photograph taken together, and at the time I found him warm, friendly and genuine.

Nearly twenty years later, in 1986, I saw him again when he was president of the United States. My aunt Marge Elerding, travel agency owner Barbara Moe and I escorted fifty-five Montanans on an Anderson-Elerding tour to New York City for the Centennial Celebration of the Statue of Liberty. During the 1980s, my aunt and I escorted numerous tours throughout the United States for A&E Travel Service.

We joined some six million people in Manhattan for the big show. In his speech that preceded the dazzling fireworks, President Reagan said that his five and a half years in the White House left him with one overriding impression of hope. "The things that unite us—America's past of which we are so proud—our hopes and aspirations for the future of the world and this much loved country," he said. "These things far outweigh what little divides us."

Innocents Abroad

In April 1970, Governor Forrest H. Anderson appointed me the Montana Ambassador of Goodwill to the International Convention of Women in Radio and Television in London, England, to which I was a delegate. I traveled with my mother. Her mother was born in Liverpool, England, and my mother was proud of her English heritage.

The conference was a wonderful adventure for a woman raised in Helena, Montana. There were delegates from the United Kingdom as well as Finland, Formosa, Germany, Greece, Holland, Hong Kong, Japan, Korea, Lebanon, Thailand, the United States and Yugoslavia.

I was hostess at a reception held at the House of Parliament. The other conference goers and I toured Queen Elizabeth II's art gallery in Buckingham Palace and met Lord Redmayne, whip of the Tory Party under four prime ministers and Director of Harrods, the largest department store in the world and the shopping place for royalty. We toured Harrods. I remember there was one entire floor with nothing but pianos on it. We also toured the backstages of numerous London theaters and music halls.

CBS President Frank Stanton and BBC Director-General Charles Curran were among convention speakers.

Norma with Governor Forrest Anderson in 1968.

The trip had special meaning for my mother as well. She was reuinted with a cousin, Grenfell Mathison, with whom she had played as a child in Liverpool. Grenfell had two daughters, one who was my age, Carol, who joined us. Several years later Carol visited me in Montana. We exchange Christmas cards every year.

As the goodwill ambassador, it was my task to present a gift to Princess Margaret on behalf of the State of Montana. The gift was a framed reproduction of *The Queen's War Hounds* by Charles

123

Russell. The painting, done in 1914, depicts an Indian in the foreground who is helping Royal Canadian Mounted Police track a fugitive. It was purchased by George Lane, prominent Canadian stockman and friend of the former Prince of Wales, who once owned the adjoining ranch. Lane presented the painting to the Province of Alberta and it now hangs in the House of Parliament in Edmonton.

A plaque on the Russell reproduction read:

The Queen's War Hounds
by C. M. Russell
Presented to H. R. H. Princess Margaret
From the State of Montana, U. S. A.
London England
April 24. 1970

Although convention delegates were to meet Princess Margaret at a reception, I had to make separate and elaborate arrangements to get the gift into the possession of the Princess. We were given permission to bring the gift to Kensington Palace, Princess Margaret's home, and present it to her lady-in-waiting, Juliet Smith.

As my mother and I drove in a cab up the long tree-lined avenue to Kensington Palace, past beautiful formal gardens, I kept thinking, what an experience this was for two women from Montana.

As we approached the palace I turned to my mother and asked, "Mother, what are you thinking?"

She replied, "I'm thinking I'm going to wet my pants!"

We both laughed. We were met at the door by Juliet Smith. She invited us into a small waiting room and she graciously accepted the gift on behalf of the Princess.

Later, I met Princess Margaret at a formal reception that was part of the convention. We were told that we were not to speak to her unless she spoke to us first and that she was to be addressed as "Ma'am." We were also taught how to curtsy.

Since I was the governor's goodwill ambassador, I decided to wear my bright yellow and blue, "I'm From Montana, the Big Sky Country" badge on my aqua and silver brocade gown. As the Princess walked slowly past each of us in the long reception line, she came to me, stopped, looked at my badge, and said, "What's that?"

She had spoken to me first, so after I had curtsied, I had the perfect opportunity to discharge my duties. "Ma'am, I'm from Montana," I blurted. "And I bring you greetings from our great state."

She smiled and walked on.

When the convention was over and I had returned to Montana, I received the first of three letters from Juliet Smith, each with the seal of Kensington Palace on them.

The first letter, dated May 1, 1970, read:

> *Dear Mrs. Ashby,*
> *I am bidden by Princess Margaret to write and thank you so much for bringing the picture which was so kindly given to the Princess by the State of Montana.*
> *Her Royal Highness was really delighted to receive this and I am writing to the Governor on her behalf.*
> *I do hope that you have been enjoying the rest of your stay in London. It was so nice meeting you and your mother when you came to Kensington Palace.*
> *Yours sincerely,*
> *Juliet Smith*
> *Lady-in-Waiting*

I wrote back a letter requesting pencil tracings of the feet of Princess Margaret's two children so a friend of mine, Mary Morgan, on the Blackfeet Reservation, could make moccasins for them. Her reply was sent on June 26, 1970:

> *Dear Mrs. Ashby,*
> *Thank you so much for your letter of the 6th June. I am afraid it is not really possible to send you tracings of the children's feet, but if it is any help their shoe sizes are:*
> *Lady Sarah   Size 12*
> *Lord Linley   Size 13*
> *Princess Margaret much appreciates your kind thought in sending these Indian Moccasins from the Blackfeet Tribe and greatly looks forward to seeing them.*
> *Yours sincerely,*
> *Juliet Smith*
> *Lady-in-Waiting.*

The final letter, dated Oct. 2, 1970, was a thank-you for the moccasins and was signed by the Lady-in-Waiting Juliet Townsend, who I believe was the same Juliet Smith with a new married name.

I wrote back a letter requesting pencil tracings of the feet of Princess Margaret's two children so a friend of mine, Mary Morgan, on the Blackfeet Reservation, could make moccasins for them.

01-930 3141

KENSINGTON PALACE
W.8

2nd October, 1970

Dear Mrs. Ashby,

    Princess Margaret has asked me to write to thank you so very much for the beautiful mocassins which you sent as a gift for her children from the Blackfeet Tribe of Montana.

    Her Royal Highness was most impressed by the skilled workmanship which had gone into the embroidering of these mocassins, and she would be grateful if you could send a special message of her appreciation to Mary Morgan for all her hard work.

    I am afraid there are certain difficulties with regard to taking a photograph of the children in the mocassins but I can assure you that they both appreciated them very much indeed.   They certainly are delightfully soft and must be extremely comfortable to wear.

Yours sincerely,

Juliet Townsend

Lady-in-Waiting

Mrs. Norma Ashby.

Women in the Services

In 1972, I was appointed by Secretary of Defense Melvin Laird to a three-year term on the Defense Advisory Committee on Women in the Services (DACOWITS). The civilian committee advises the Department of Defense on matters and policies relating to women in the services and promotes public awareness of military service as a career for women. It was an exciting time, as it was near the end of the time when the women in the military were separated from the men in groups associated with the different branches of the military. The WAVES were part of the Navy; the WACS, the Army; and the WAF, the Air Force. Later, these separate groups were integrated into the regular Navy, Army and Air Force.

We visited bases throughout the nation—from Florida to Colorado—as each of our biennial meetings was hosted by a different branch of the service. We also had meetings at the Pentagon and at Walter Reed Army Medical of Center in Washington, D. C.

One of the highlights of my service on this committee happened during a reception with First Lady Pat Nixon in 1974. A charming and gracious first lady, she greeted each of us as a photographer snapped our picture. I asked her about a C. M. Russell bronze I had seen during our tour of the White House and we talked about the possibility of a showing of Russell works in the White House, though this did not come to pass.

During my tenure, I also had an opportunity to interview Secretary of Defense Elliot Richardson in the Pentagon's TV studios. Before the interview, Secretary Richardson told me about a skiing vacation he and his family had taken in Glacier National Park. When the camera began to roll, we had a good visit about the duties of his office and I brought the tape home to play on *Today in Montana*.

Three months later, President Richard Nixon appointed Secretary Richardson as his new attorney general. I sent him a thank-you and wished him well in his new assignment and enclosed some dry flies my husband had tied. In his letter back to me, he wrote, "Thanks for the two Grey Wolf flies. I look forward to using them at the earliest opportunity, although I am afraid my new duties will not leave much time for fishing or for a delightful trip to Montana."

During my time on the committee, I organized a banquet to honor Montana's military women with the help of Zonta, a women's service club of professional and executive women. We held the First Salute banquet at Malmstrom Air Force Base in 1973 and Brigadier General Ann Hoefly, Chief of the Air Force Nurse Corps, was our

---

One of the highlights of my service on this committee happened during a reception with First Lady Pat Nixon in 1974. A charming and gracious first lady, she greeted each of us as a photographer snapped our picture.

ABOVE: Brigadier General Ann Hoefly, chief of the Air Force Nurse Corps and Norma on June 1, 1973. General Hoefly was speaker at the First Salute to Montana's Military Women Banquet.

BELOW: Secretary of Defense Elliott Richardson and Norma doing an interview in the Pentagon broadcast studio in 1973.

guest speaker. I interviewed her on *Today in Montana*. She talked about the expanding role for women nurses in the Air Force from conducting well-baby and cancer-detection clinics to home visits. Our Second Salute was in 1974 at Malmstrom Air Force Base and our speaker was Colonel Billie Bobbitt, Director of Women in the Air Force, who said, "Military service provides an excellent opportunity to young women for education, training, equal pay, challenging jobs and progress."

Of the forty women I served with during my three year term in DACOW-ITS, one in particular remains a close friend to this day. She is Ebby Halliday Acers of Dallas, Texas. She is a vibrant, ninety-three-year-old real estate mogul. Ebby founded Ebby Halliday Realtors, the top locally owned residential real estate brokerage in Dallas, not to mention Texas, with twenty-seven offices and 1,200 agents. She goes to work every day and keeps two secretaries busy managing her schedule. She contributes time and money to causes she cares about. As well as a close personal friend, she continues to be a major influence and source of inspiration in my life.

Paul Harvey in Cascade

When the Cascade High School class of 1976 told their class sponsor Bill Cornelius in 1975 that they wanted ABC radio commentator Paul Harvey as their commencement speaker the following year, Bill said he would look into it. He contacted Paul's office in Chicago and learned his speaking fee was $5,000, an impossible amount for the class to raise. However, the idea of having Paul Harvey speak in Cascade during the bicentennial caught fire and the townspeople were all for it. Bill found out that Harvey's speaking fee would go up in 1976, so Bill and his wife Shirley put up their own money to cover the fee. Paul accepted their invitation to speak in Cascade.

On Saturday, June 26, 1976, Paul Harvey flew his own plane into the Great Falls International Airport that morning and was driven by Jeep to Cascade.

He arrived in time for Cascade's Bicentennial Parade, which featured marching bands, floats and lots of horses. The men all had grown beards and the women were dressed in bicentennial dresses.

Paul cruised down the main street of Cascade, population 740, in an open antique car. As the co-chair of the Cascade County Bicentennial Commission, I had the privilege of sitting behind Paul. He was a merry, handsome man wearing a white hat, and as we moved along, he asked me in that famous deep voice to whisper to him the names of people I knew along the parade route. When I spotted my mother, Ella Mehmke, I told him her name and he waved and yelled, "Hello, Ella." She was thrilled!

Following the parade, he was invited to a luncheon at the log home along the Missouri River of Ken and Marion Gilbert. Ken was co-chair of the Cascade Bicentennial Committee with Bob Woody. He had planted radishes in his garden in the shape of the words, "Hello Paul."

Radio commentator Paul Harvey with Norma in Cascade, Montana, on June 26, 1976, where Paul was the featured speaker for the bicentennial celebration.

Norma in the bicentennial parade in Great Falls on July 3, 1976.

That afternoon, Paul Harvey entered the Cascade High School playing field to an estimated crowd of 3,000 men, women and children. The crowds sat on bleachers and on the grass.

Each of these people paid $7.50 a ticket, which admitted them to the speech as well as to a beef barbeque afterward. Nine area ranchers donated the beef. The steaks and hamburgers were grilled on a seventy-five foot long grill, which was constructed on cinder blocks. Potatoes were cooked over coals in a giant pit that was dug. Large plastic bags full of homemade salad were dished up along with rolls and beverages. It was a feast.

People had come from everywhere in Montana and the nation, especially those who had once lived in Cascade. It far surpassed the town's expectations and the Corneliuses were repaid. After expenses, the profits were between $12,000 and $14,000, which were given to the library and Senior Citizens Center.

Following his visit, Paul wrote a tribute to Cascade, which he delivered on the air Monday, June 28, 1976. Here is the tribute as it was reprinted in the *Cascade Courier*:

Over My Shoulder a Backward Glance

But what can a town of 740 populations do to celebrate the Bicentennial?

Well, I'll tell you what one did.

The Missouri River, up near its beginning, has worn a pass through the Big Belt Mountains in Montana.

And sitting in that saddle alongside the River is the town of Cascade, Montana—population 740.

Stunted by cold and heat, nourished by cattle and wheat, Cascade has a blink-and-you've-missed-it downtown.

Yet Saturday I rode through that town in a parade one hour and two miles long!

Ninety units rolling or riding or marching.

One of the brass bands came 400 miles to participate.

Former hometowners came from as far as Florida.

So three thousand watched that parade in a town of 740—then converged on the athletic field for a barbecue afterward.

I took no pictures I can show you, but some precious mental snapshots I can share.

Ken Gilbert's retirement cabin of logs overlooking the river—and in his garden—"Welcome Paul" spelled out in radishes.

Working cowboys in my Arizona desert wear slick leather chaps to deflect cactus and chaparral.

Working Wyoming cowboys wear Angora wool chaps to keep warm.

Cascade, Montana is thirty years behind the times in ways that we all ought to be.

Sales clerks are still polite and pleasant.

It's like a bold step backward through time for a fugitive from the city to have his jet met by a jeep.

To enter the festival grounds by stagecoach.

And fun!

Shirley Cornelius will tell you a unit of the parade took a wrong turn-

In a town six blocks long they got lost and turned left and haven't been heard from since.

And that's the truth—If not the "whole" truth.

Then there's the prettiest face in town worn by a young woman named Connie Fleschenhar. She constantly spreads

> "Stunted by cold and heat, nourished by cattle and wheat, Cascade has a blink-and-you've-missed-it downtown. Yet Saturday I rode through that town in a parade one hour and two miles long!"

such a contagious smile from her wheelchair that folks who do not have M.S. and aren't smiling are reminded to.

I'm making many trips this Bicentennial year—Louisville today, three and four every week—but none other to a town as tiny as Cascade, Montana.

Yet if most of my other recollections become a blur of airports and Holiday Inns and Coca Cola signs—those precious hours Saturday will not soon be forgot.

The senior citizens of the county got special seating for the events of the day—authentic pioneers these—trappers, miners, homesteaders, cowboys, and the women who shared it all.

The lush green years and the long, rough winters.

Nobody ever went to Cascade, Montana to sit in the shade and sponge off somebody else; neither the founders nor their heirs.

When the military fly-by had flown by,

When the Governor had had his say and it was time for the lady who so masterfully mistressed the ceremonies to call it a day, she—Frieda Jones—waved toward the posted American colors—that feminine substitute for a salute—both dainty and definite—

And she said

And I quote:

"From yonder beyond the mountains we have been called provincial. To those who so kindly describe us, I say thank you. And please. God, let us stay that way for a blessed little while."

Endquote

And I was sitting right up front.

And I swear, the flag waved back!

Art for Sale: The C.M. Russell Auction

Of all of the committees and projects I have been involved in, the most dear to my heart is the C.M. Russell Auction of Original Western Art. This thirty-six-year-old, world-famous auction that draws annual crowds of up to 1,200 people, plus thousands of western art to Great Falls, does an annual business of over a million dollars. It has been described by the National Geographic as an event that "in one brief weekend, turns Charlie's hometown into one of the world's most lucrative art markets."

And it was an event that almost didn't happen.

> "I'm making many trips this bicentennial year—Louisville today, three and four every week—but none other to a town as tiny as Cascade, Montana."

In 1968 the Advertising Club of Great Falls (now the Great Falls Advertising Federation) was looking for a new fund-raiser. Their annual fund-raiser called the Cadillac Dinner—where a Cadillac was given away to a lucky ticket holder—had to be discontinued when, as part of his statewide crackdown on gambling, Attorney General Bob Woodahl declared the fund-raiser a lottery.

Three years earlier, on September 25, 1965, I went with auctioneer Barney Sparrow and his wife Claris to the estate auction of Abbie Welch in Geraldine, Montana. Held in the Geraldine High School gymnasium, the auction featured the oriental rugs, antique furniture and cut glass from her home. It was my first auction and from the first item to the final bid, I was enthralled. Barney did a great job with his chant and the bids were rapid. I even bought a small cut glass candy dish for $7.50.

This was where I came up with the idea of an auction for the Ad Club's new fund-raiser. An auction, it seemed to me, had all the qualities we were looking for: excitement, suspense, color, crowds, fun and profit. Then I wondered what kind of an auction we would have. That's when I thought of the citizen who has brought more fame to our city than anyone else—cowboy artist Charles Russell. Why not a C. M. Russell Auction of Original Western Art, I thought, for the benefit of the Russell gallery (which is now the C.M. Russell Museum) and the Ad Club of Great Falls as well? I thought of J. Frank Dobie, who wrote that "no state in the Union has been affected by one man as has Montana by Charley Russell."

Through the years I did many interviews about the life and work of Charles Russell. But in all the books, articles, and films which talk about Russell, I think his own words from the introduction to his book, *Trails Plowed Under*, describe him best. These were written just a few months before his death in 1926.

Norma with Fred Renner, first honorary chairman; and Sam Gilluly, director, Montana Historical Society; at the first C. M. Russell Auction on March 6, 1969.

Head table at the Chuckwagon Brunch of the first Russell auction on March 6, 1969. From left: Sam Gilluly, Fred Renner, Terry Melton, director of the C. M. Russell Gallery; LeRoy Stahl, Advertising Club of Great Falls member; Jack Raty, auctioneer; Kenny Mortag, auction clerk; and John McLaughlin, Great Falls mayor. Photo by Dale Burk.

A Few Words About Myself...

The papers have been kind to me—many times more kind than true. Although I worked for many years on the range, I am not what the people think a cowboy should be. I was neither a good roper nor rider. I was a night wrangler. How good I was, I'll leave it for the people I worked for to say—there are still a few of them living. In the spring I wrangled horses, in the fall I herded beef. I worked for the big outfits and always held my job.

I have many friends among cowmen and cowpunchers. I have always been what is called a good mixer—I had friends when I had nothing else. My friends were not always within the law, but I haven't said how law-abiding I was myself. I haven't been too bad nor too good to get along with.

Life has never been too serious with me—I lived to play and I'm playing yet. Laughs and good judgment have saved me many a black eye, but I don't laugh at other's tears. I was a wild young man, but age has made me gentle. I drank, but never alone, and when I drank it was no secret. I am still friendly with drinking men.

My friends are mixed—preachers, priests, and sinners. I belong to no church but am friendly toward and respect all of them. I have always liked horses and since I was eight years old have always owned a few.

I am old-fashioned and peculiar in my dress. I am eccentric. (That is a polite way of saying you're crazy.) I believe in luck and have had lots of it.

To have talent is no credit to its owner; what man can't help he should get neither credit for nor blame for—it's not his fault. I am an illustrator. There are lots better ones, but some worse. Any man that can make a living doing what he likes is lucky, and I'm that. Any time I cash in now, I win.

Charles M. Russell
Great Falls, Montana

When I presented the idea for the Russell auction to the Ad Club's board of directors, they gave me this surprising response. Who, they asked, would want to honor a dead artist?

I was so convinced that it would work that I called of my two friends, Ad Club President Bill Samson and another Ad Club member, Tom Johnson. The three of us brainstormed. We decided the auction would not only honor Charlie but would also be a showcase to introduce and promote new and contemporary Western artists. When it was presented in that way, the board approved it and we were on our way.

Tom Johnson was named first chairman and dozens of Ad Clubbers signed up for all the jobs that needed to be done.

In fewer than three months, the Ad Club launched the first C. M. Russell Auction of Original Western Art on March 6, 1969, at the Rainbow Hotel. March was chosen because Russell was born on March 19, 1864. Called the "Biggest Whingding in Ad Club History," four hundred western art enthusiasts attended

Cowboy artist Charles M. Russell, 1864 to 1926, in his Great Falls studio, the namesake of the C. M. Russell Auction.

from twenty-one Montana towns and seven states. Twenty-six artists participated and seventy-seven works of art were sold. The auction gross was $20,160 with $10,872 donated to the Russell Gallery.

Several key people contributed to the success of the auction. Fred Renner, foremost authority on Charles Russell, was our first honorary chairman. He gave us his list of those interested in Russell. Many of those names proved to be some of our best art buyers and auction supporters. During March, an exhibit of twenty-one original Russell paintings, watercolors and pen and ink drawings from the Renner Collection were displayed at the Montana Bank in Great Falls.

On the inside cover of the eight-page auction catalogue, Fred Renner said:

No citizen has brought more honor to Great Falls, Montana than Charles Marion Russell. This was his home town for more than thirty years. It was in his studio here that his great artistic talents were devoted to recording the life of our pioneers with love and deep understanding. His was a living legacy to those who have followed; the painters, sculptors, writers, and all others dedicated to preserving our western heritage. To most of these, Charles Marion Russell will always be the greatest of all western artists.

It is significant, therefore, that the first C. M. Russell Auction of Original Western Art is to be held in Great Falls. This is for the benefit of the C. M. Russell Gallery, which has one of the finest collections of his work. I wish to personally commend the Advertising Club of Great Falls for spearheading this major art event.

Dr. Van Kirke Nelson of Kalispell, a western art dealer and collector who had been involved in western art auctions in his area,

Bill Samson, president, Advertising Club of Great Falls; Norma and Tom Johnson, first Russell Auction chairman, holding Branson Stevenson etchings of Russell studio in 1970.

gave us invaluable help in establishing a workable format and provided us with contacts as well as art work for the auction.

We found our auctioneer, Jack Raty of Fort Shaw, through my husband, Shirley, who had heard him do farm sales in Montana. Tom Johnson, Bill Samson and I met with Jack in the Rainbow Hotel coffee shop and asked him to sell the sugar bowl on the table. He immediately went into his rapid chant and we hired him on the spot. Although he was primarily a livestock and farm equipment auctioneer, the people loved Jack's colorful western appearance, personality and style and they responded with their bids. When he retired in 1996 at the 28th Russell auction, he made this announcement, "My first auction sale I had coming out of auction school was a 4-H baby beef sale in Fort Benton, Montana. I sold that sale for twenty-seven years before I turned it over to somebody else. Tonight will be my twenty-seventh year here at the Russell auction selling for the Ad Club and you folks and it's time for me to give it up and let some other auctioneer take it over." Bruce Brock of LeMars, Iowa, who won titles as World Champion Auctioneer and International Champion Auctioneer, has ably served as our auctioneer since Jack retired.

At the first Russell auction, I was given this award which I treasure to this day:

> Advertising Club of Great Falls presents this Certificate of Recognition to Norma Ashby for originating and masterminding the first annual C. M. Russell Auction of Original Western Art, thereby opening a new era for the C. M. Russell Gallery, the Advertising Club and the City of Great Falls. We hereby extend our appreciation of her creativity and sincere effort in making this project a success. Presented this Sixth day of March, 1969 Tom Johnson, Project Chairman Bill Samson, President

From 1969 to 2004, the Russell auction has sold more than $17 million of western art, $4 million of which has been donated to the C. M. Russell Museum. The auction started off with seventy-seven pieces by twenty-six artists in 1969; in 2004, the auction had grown to 319 pieces. In the auction's first thirty-six years, the highest price paid for a work of art was in 2002, when $240,000 was paid for a C. M. Russell watercolor, *Waiting*, that was donated by an anonymous buyer to the C. M. Russell Museum for its permanent collection.

The eight-page, black-and-white catalog in 1969 has grown to a

---

We found our auctioneer, Jack Raty of Fort Shaw, through my husband, Shirley, who had heard him do farm sales in Montana. Tom Johnson, Bill Samson and I met with Jack in the Rainbow Hotel coffee shop and asked him to sell the sugar bowl on the table.

196-page full-color catalog in 2004. Auction ticket prices have risen from $7.50 for the one-day event in 1969 to up to $175 in 2004. Only two artists have been juried into all the Russell auctions since it started: Steve Seltzer of Great Falls and Bob Morgan of Helena. Until 1976, the Russell auction was held at the Rainbow Hotel; after that it has been housed at the Heritage Inn, which has been its home ever since.

The Scriver Bronze, a buffalo skull, the symbol Russell used along with his name in signing his works, was initially given to someone who had a special association with Russell. The first Scriver Bronze, which was given in perpetuity by the late Browning sculptor Bob Scriver, was presented to Jack Russell, son of Charlie Russell, and his wife Lucille in 1970. Later it was given to someone who has contributed to the Russell auction or to the field of western art. I was totally taken by surprise when I was the recipient of the Scriver Bronze in 1993. It is among my most treasured awards.

During the second year of the auction, in 1970, we launched the "I Like Charlie Russell Because..." essay contest among fifth graders, the year Montana history is taught, was launched. The Ad Club wanted children to learn about Charlie Russell, the Russell Museum and our auction. More than 23,000 fifth graders have participated in the contest from public and parochial schools in Great Falls and throughout Cascade County since then. The city and county winners would read their essays on *Today in Montana* and continue to read them at the auction's Chuckwagon Brunch. I am always amazed at the quality of their writing and the poise these ten- and eleven-year-olds have in speaking to an audience of more than 1,000 people. One of my favorite statements about Charlie was written by Josh Canada from Cascade. He said, "I like Charlie Russell because I know talent when I see it."

An important aspect of the Russell auction are the artists and dealers who have exhibited work. In 1972 the exhibit room directory had twenty-four exhibitors, In 2004 there were more than 100. The Russell auction has brought colorful and knowledgeable western art people to Great Falls, many of whom have been guests on *Today in Montana*, including Noah "Pidg" Beery, Malcolm. S. "Bud" McKay, Victor Hammer, John Clymer, Bob Morgan, Steve Seltzer, George Montgomery, Denver Pyle, Fred and Ginger Renner, Bob Rockwell, Slim Pickens, Charley and Rozene Pride, Jack and Lucille Russell and Bill Sherman.

The success of the auction has been a wonderful thing to witness. It has come from the hard work and cooperation of the Ad Club, the

---

One of my favorite statements about Charlie was written by Josh Canada from Cascade. He said, "I like Charlie Russell because I know talent when I see it."

C. M. Russell Museum, the artists and dealers, the patrons and the local, national and international media. It springs from the deep love and appreciation that people have for the work of Charles Russell, whether they are fellow artists or simply appreciative onlookers.

People ask me if I ever tire of being involved in the Russell auction after all these years. My answer is no. I am as enthused about the auction today as when it started in 1969. I am particularly thrilled with new members of Ad Club who are doing a great job of stepping forward to take leadership roles in the event. The auction will be around for many years to come.

In 1970, I interviewed Jack Russell, the adopted son of Charlie and Nancy Russell and his wife Lucille. The Russells had traveled from Oceanside, California, to Great Falls to attend the second C.M. Russell auction where Jack was to receive the first Scriver Bronze.

Jack was a very reserved and soft-spoken man and Lucille was a small, smiling woman. I was such a fan of Charlie Russell, I think I expected Jack to be some kind of reincarnation of his father. I learned a hard lesson. No one should ever be compared to anyone else. Jack was his own person. Charlie was larger than life for all of us who love his work and the stories surrounding him.

Jack was adopted by the Russells in 1916 when he was a baby and he had not been back to Great Falls in thirty years. The last time he was in town was to bury his mother, Nancy Russell, in 1940. He told me he planned to visit the cemetery, so I mentioned that people were always impressed with the roughness of his father's tombstone. "It is a big boulder," he said.

I asked him if he remembered the occasion of his father's funeral in 1926, when people lined the streets of Great Falls to watch the horse-drawn hearse go by and to pay tribute to the cowboy artist. He said he was ten years old at the time and he talked about the procession with the horse-drawn hearse, followed by a horse with an empty saddle, according to his father's wishes.

When his father was alive, Jack climbed on Charlie's lap and had him tell stories and he also went into the studio to watch him paint.

I mentioned that one of the qualities people enjoyed most about Charlie was his tremendous sense of humor. I asked him if this came across to him when he was growing up. "Yes," Jack said. "That and his kindness."

Jack said Charlie never got mad when Jack occasionally brought his playmates into the studio. "Mother got disturbed occasionally," he added. "But Dad didn't."

After Russell's death, I asked Jack if he spent time at Bull Head

> *People ask me if I ever tire of being involved in the Russell auction after all these years. My answer is no. I am as enthused about the auction today as when it started in 1969.*

Lodge, the Russell's cabin at Lake McDonald. He said the last time he and his mother had been there was in the summer of 1935.

When I asked him if he had any of Russell's original work, he said, "I don't have any originals." He said in the settlement of the estate, he was not included "in that way" and he had to make a living and couldn't afford original artwork of Russell's.

At that time, there was quite a controversy raging in Great Falls about the old Russell home. Although it was saved eventually through the efforts of the Montana Federation of Garden Clubs and is now open to the public, at that time some people thought it should be torn down to make room for a park. I asked Jack if he had any feelings one way or another.

> I think the people of Great Falls and Montana are doing a very fine job with the museum and the memories, and I don't think it's up to me to make any comment on how they do this. I think the job is being beautifully done.

Jack, who said he was going to see the house and other old haunts while he was in town, said he went to Whittier Grade School. Then, when Russell died, he said, "we moved to California and I was in public schools most of the time." Later he went to Pasadena City College and the University of Southern California. Since then, he said he had worked on "highways, surveys, construction and design."

I showed him a very rare picture I had that was loaned to me by the Russell studio, (the precursor of the C.M. Russell Museum). Nancy Russell was holding baby Jack in her arms. Fred Renner, a Russell authority who had probably seen every Russell photo around, had never seen it. I showed it to Jack, who hadn't even seen it himself.

Then I turned to Mrs. Russell, who had a fascinating hobby that was in keeping with the western theme established by Russell. She had made a rug for Jack that featured a buffalo skull using punch work, which, she said, was "a lot of hard work and pleasure." The rug is now in their den at home.

When I asked Jack what his reaction was when he saw the Russell symbol of the skull, he said, "I'm so proud of that. It's a beautiful thing."

A Fish for Montana

In the summer of 1976, my husband and I were driving back to Great Falls from our cabin near Lincoln. I was looking at a Montana

State Highway map that showed the symbols of Montana on it I noted that there was no state fish. Both ardent fly fishermen, we wondered why this symbol had been overlooked. That's when I launched, with the endorsement of Nels Thoreson of the Montana Fish and Game Department in Great Falls, a statewide campaign for a state fish on *Today in Montana*.

Two candidates were proposed by Nels: the blackspotted cutthroat trout and the Montana grayling, although other nominations were encouraged. Both species were on the threatened list. We felt that if we could draw attention to this fish, perhaps its conditions could be improved.

Nels helped us develop criteria for a state fish. The fish had to be native to Montana. It couldn't be adopted by another state as a state fish. The fish had to be accepted (popular) by the people It had to be a game fish that was distinctive in appearance, and it had to be found in more than one area of the state.

Dr. Louis Hagener, head of the science department at Northern Montana College and his wife Toni, curator of the H. Earl Clack Museum in Havre, supported the blackspotted cutthroat trout. They observed that in addition to meeting all of the requirements we had set forth, the cutthroat enhanced Montana's image as a fisherman's paradise of clean, clear, sparkling waters. The Hageners also pointed out that the fish bears Captain William Clark's name (*Salmo clarkii*). Clark identified the fish when he and Captain Meriwether Lewis and the Corps of Discovery reached the Great Falls of the Missouri on their westward journey in 1805. Captain Lewis wrote in his journal on June 13, 1805, "These trout (caught in the falls) are from 16 to 23 inches in length, precisely resemble our mountain or speckled trout in form and the position of their fins, but the specks on these are of a deep black instead of the red or goald colour (sic) of those common in the United States."

Governor Tom Judge and Norma holding mounted blackspotted cutthroat trout, Montana's state fish. Representative George Johnston of Cut Bank and senator Margaret Warden of Great Falls carried the bill for the state fish in the 1977 Montana State Legislature.

Norma in her Princess Thunder Woman dress in 1982.

Of the nearly 1,000 votes for twenty-three species of fish that came in from sixty-four Montana towns and four states, the blackspotted cutthroat trout received 520 votes, easily outdistancing the Montana grayling's 200 votes. The rainbow trout placed third with 107 votes.

Senator Margaret Warden of Great Falls and Representative George Johnston of Cut Bank introduced the bill nominating a state fish during the forty-fifth Legislature in 1977. The bill passed by wide margins in both houses. Senator Warden, one of Montana's 220,000 resident fishermen, called the blackspotted cutthroat trout "a fighting, good-eating, and beautiful fish."

Art Whitney of the Montana Department of Fish and Game agreed:

> Naming the blackspotted cutthroat trout as Montana's State Fish is just another indication that the people in this state will settle for nothing but the very best in protecting the way of life we are all dedicated to preserving.

On February 10, 1977, Governor Thomas Judge signed the law designating the blackspotted cutthroat trout (*Salmo clarki*) as Montana's official state fish. As a thank-you, I presented him with a mounted blackspotted cutthroat trout to hang in his office.

Contest Winner

One of the most fun contests I have ever won—and I've won some dandies, including the Cow Chip Throwing Contest and the Milker With the Most Pull in the City Folks Division at the State Fair—was the Best Western Character Contest, sponsored by the Cascade County Mental Health Association in 1982.

I entered the contest in my Indian dress as Princess Thunder Woman. There were four other contestants: a schoolmarm, a soldier from the Seventh Calvary, Miss Kitty from the TV show *Gunsmoke,* and a mountain man.

The one who raised the most money for the Association's fund-raiser, the Mile of Quarters, got to appear in cartoonist Stan Lynde's comic strip,

Latigo, and receive the original strip. I was the lucky winner and Stan's original strip featuring Thunder Woman is in a prominent place in our family room.

From the Bitterroot to Bluebunch Wheatgrass: Montana Symbols

In 1989, I realized that the *Symbols of Montana* booklet, produced thirteen years earlier by Rex C. Myers and the Montana Historical Society in association with the Helena Kiwanis Club, was out of date. A number of new symbols had been added. For Montana's Centennial in 1989, I updated the booklet and Jim Kittredge of Advanced Litho Printing in Great Falls designed it.

We sent free copies of the booklet to all public and private libraries around the state, including the Burlington Northern Foundation, Montana history enthusiast Bill Sherman, Delta Kappa Gamma International Society (Alpha Mu, Montana State Chapter), Montana Historical Society Foundation and School Superintendent Nancy Keenan. The symbols are an interesting illustration of the historic development of Montana and of what was important to Montanans. Montana's first symbol, the state seal that bears the motto *oro y plata,* or gold and silver, reflects Montana's gold- and silver-mining past. Later, symbols such as the flower, the song and the bird represented what was near and dear to the hearts of Montanans. Montana has adopted a total of thirteen symbols that represent the economics, interests and affections of its citizens.

Stan Lynde's original comic strip featuring Princes Thunder Woman, Norma's prize for winning the Mile of Quarters fund-raiser for the Cascade County Mental Health Association in 1982.

The following is a list of the thirteen state symbols, and the dates they were adopted by the legislature, all of which appear in the book, except the state butterfly, which was added to the list in 2002.

Seal, 1895. In addition to the motto, it contains the Great Falls of the Missouri, a rising sun, mountains, forests, a pick, shovel and plow.

Flower, 1895. The bitterroot

Flag, 1905. Blue with Montana above the state seal in Helvetica bold letters.

Bird, 1931. The western meadowlark.

State Song, 1945. "Montana," with lyrics by Charles C. Cohan and melody by Joseph E. Howard. It was first presented in Butte in 1910.

Tree, 1949. The ponderosa pine.

Gemstones, 1969. Sapphire and agate.

Grass, 1973. Bluebunch wheatgrass.

Fish, 1977. The blackspotted cutthroat trout.

Animal, 1982. The grizzly bear.

Ballad, 1983. "Montana Melody," with lyrics by LeGrande and Carleen Harvey of Missoula, melody by LeGrande Harvey.

Fossil, 1985. The duck-billed dinosaur (*Maiasaura peeblesorum*)

Butterfly, 2002. The Mourning Cloak.

Celebrations

Montanans love to celebrate. And I am no exception. Since 1964, when Governor Tim Babcock appointed me to the Montana Territorial Centennial Commission, I have been involved in various celebrations with people I often featured on *Today in Montana*.

That year, the Montana Centennial Train—organized by Howard Kelsey, Montana dude rancher—carried 300 Montanans to the World's Fair in New York to promote our celebration. Women, including me, wore outfits made by Margaret Schmidt of Fort Harrison. She used dyed sheets to make long skirts with bustles and she applied feathers, flowers and chiffon to create beautiful hats. She never sewed, she used safety pins and straight pins to hold the costumes together and it worked! When she retired as a milliner, Margaret gave me her collection of hats.

I invited John Steinbeck, who had won the Pulitzer Prize for *The Grapes of Wrath* and the Nobel Prize for Literature in 1962, to

---

That year, the Montana Centennial Train—organized by Howard Kelsey, a Montana dude rancher—carried 300 Montanans to the World's Fair in New York to promote our celebration. Women, including me, wore outfits made by Margaret Schmidt of Fort Harrison.

attend the Montana Territorial Centennial Train Dinner at the Commodore Hotel. I knew of his love for Montana from reading his book, *Travels with Charley*. He wrote: "I am in love with Montana. For other states I have admiration, respect, recognition, even some affection, but with Montana, it is love...Montana has a spell on me. It is grandeur and warmth. If Montana had a seacoast, or if I could live away from the sea, I would instantly move there and petition for admission. Of all the states it is my favorite and my love."

I thought if he was free he might join us...Here is his hand-written reply dated April 20, 1964:

> *Dear Norma Beatty:*
> *Please tell the delegation I think they're crazy to leave Montana for New York but as long as they have, I sure do bid them welcome and wish I could be there to do it personally. If I'd known about it earlier, I'd have made certain of it.*
>
> *I hope the delegates enjoy New York, but please go home before you're hooked. New York can be bad that way. I know people who came for a weekend twenty years ago.*
>
> *Some one told me you are moving the Pacific Ocean right up to the edge of the Bitterroot Range. I hope you'll let me know when you get it all poured because then you will have everything. Of course it's a little hard on Seattle and Portland, but what the hell! They'll only be a little damper than they are now.*
>
> *Anyway—greetings and have a good time.*
> *Yours, John Steinbeck*

In 1976, Governor Tom Judge appointed me to the Montana Bicentennial Commission, and I co-chaired the Cascade County Bicentennial Committee with Jack Moore. Montana had more planned activities than the original thirteen colonies! We had thirteen town meetings in Great Falls. We had a giant parade, chaired by Richard "Klem" Klemencic and featuring postal trucks filled with mail driving in formation down Central Avenue. We buried a time capsule in Gibson Park and filled scrapbooks with photos and clippings that were housed in the Great Falls Public Library. We planted a pine tree in Odd Fellows Park honoring Captain Robert V. Willett, Jr., USAF pilot, the only Cascade County serviceman who was missing in action in Vietnam in 1969. The state time capsule, which was a two-cubic-foot aluminum container, was filled with two

---

[Steinbeck] wrote: "I am in love with Montana. For other states I have admiration, respect, recognition, even some affection, but with Montana, it is love...Montana has a spell on me."

> *The state time capsule, which was a two-cubic-foot aluminum container, was filled with two items from each county in the state and placed in storage at the Montana Historical Society in Helena. It is to be opened one year before the tricentennial in 2075.*

items from each county in the state and placed in storage at the Montana Historical Society in Helena. It is to be opened one year before the tricentennial in 2075. Our items were a vial of water from Giant Springs and a vial of wheat from one of our county's wheat fields.

I co-chaired, with Jay Egan, the Great Falls Centennial in 1984. The celebration featured a "We the People" parade that attracted hundreds of participants and thousands of spectators on the Fourth of July. We planted trees along River Drive and saw a giant American flag installed at Overlook Park. There was a re-enactment of the Lewis and Clark's portage around the Great Falls of the Missouri, a giant mural by Robert Orduno depicting the portage unveiled in the Great Falls International Airport, scrapbooks filled with photos and clippings and an above-ground time capsule placed in the Great Falls Public Library Montana Room. I produced a video about the celebration, written by Jane Meyer and narrated by long-time radio broadcaster Dave Wilson, which was named "TV Program of the Year" by the Montana Broadcasters Association.

I helped celebrate Montana's centennial in 1989 in several ways. I helped organize—with Dick Martin, chairman of the 89ers and the Great Falls Statehood Centennial Committee—town meetings, a centennial ball in the Four Seasons with everyone in costume, and a giant parade.

I also helped to establish the tradition of the Montana Statehood Centennial bell. President Benjamin Harrison signed the proclamation declaring Montana the forty-first state in the Union at exactly 10:40 a.m. on November 8, 1889. For Montana's centennial in 1989, I planned a statewide bell-ringing ceremony to be held at that exact minute. Small Montana Heritage Bells made of solid polished brass by Creative Casting in Lewistown were distributed statewide for the ceremony. The bells had a handle shaped like the state of Montana with the Montana Centennial logo on one side of the handle and on the other side these words were engraved: "Montana 100 years old, 10:40 a.m. November 8, 1989."

The centerpiece of the ceremony was a large bell I located on a farm near Power, Montana. Originally from St. Ignatius, the bell was owned by Brent Bliss, who donated it to us in honor of his late father, Elmer Bliss. Roger Hanson, of Great Falls, painted the bell gold, and Guy Tabacco & Sons of Black Eagle built a frame for the bell. Senator Gene Thayer of Great Falls successfully sponsored a bill which was passed in the Legislature supporting our bid to place the bell in the capitol.

Transporting the heavy mounted bell to Helena for the bell-ringing ceremony was a major task. Scotty Zion of Great Falls, who had probably moved more major objects, including houses, grain silos and bridges than anyone in Montana, was the right man for the job. He placed it in front of the Capitol and on November 8, 1989 at 10:40 a.m., Governor Stan Stephens rang the giant bell for one minute as Montanans around the state joined him by ringing the small Montana Heritage Bells. Church bells, fire sirens and car horns joined in. After the ceremony, the bell was placed on the balcony overlooking the Capitol rotunda where it remains today.

In 1990, the Montana Statehood Centennial Bell award was established to perpetuate Statehood Day and to honor the best Montana history teacher of the year. Sponsored by the Montana Television Network and the Sons & Daughters of Montana Pioneers, I have coordinated the award since it began. Nominated teachers are chosen by their principals and must submit essays describing their approach to teaching Montana history. The winning teacher and her

Norma with the Montana Statehood Centennial bell in the State Capitol in Helena on the 100th birthday of Montana on November 8, 1989.

or his class travel to Helena on November 8 to ring the bell in the Capitol. The prize is $1,250 to buy Montana history materials for their school and to defray travel expenses.

In 2002, I helped coordinate publicity for the 100th anniversary of our Capitol in Helena. The celebration included a parade with Governor Judy Martz as parade marshal, a special reception in the Capitol rotunda, a dance at the Colonial Inn and festivities on the Capitol grounds which included a spectacular laser light show. The restoration of the Capitol to its original splendor was the highlight as Montanans marveled at the renewed beauty of the state's most historic building.

I have always enjoyed volunteering my time for worthwhile causes and celebrations. I like being an organizer and working with dedicated people who are instrumental in making a project a success. I like celebrations because you plan them, they happen and then they are over. All of these projects have provided me with opportunities to share my talents, develop friendships, provide lasting reminders and improvements. They have also given me memories to cherish.

—6—
Moving On

The *Today in Montana* show was my love letter to the people of Montana.

The first ten and a half years when we were a local one-hour program on KRTV in Great Falls, we developed a staff and contributors to the show who became a family. Then when *Today in Montana* reached out to the rest of the state as a thirty-minute show, we developed a new staff and new contributors and we had a new and expanded audience.

But after twenty-six and a half years at KRTV in Great Falls, I made the decision to end my television career. In some ways it was an agonizing decision because I had enjoyed my work and the people I worked with so much. On the other hand, there had been two major changes in ownership in the last four years and with those changes, my job had changed. I was still able to do local interviews and public service programming, but I found myself doing more special projects that took me away from what I loved most, which was interviewing people from around the state and around the nation.

I was proud to have a career in television. Television is much maligned—often, I think, because it is so much a part of our daily lives. But it is one of our greatest sources of news, weather and sports, whether it is an anthrax scare, an impending hurricane or the Super Bowl. None of us will ever forget, for example, how the media tied us together during the tragedy on September 11, 2001. The media is always there, through the good times and the bad, and the great thing about America is that we have the freedom to watch, to read and to listen to the things that are happening in the world around us.

In the quarter century in which I worked in television, I saw the medium change drastically. More and more local stations were being bought by large conglomerates, which meant that programming was

---

In the quarter century in which I worked in television, I saw the medium change drastically. More and more local stations were being bought by large conglomerates, which meant that programming was formulated from distant cities....

> *None of us will ever forget, for example, how the media tied us together during the tragedy on September 11, 2001. The media is always there, through the good times and the bad....*

formulated from distant cities and the local stations no longer had as much control over programming as I did back when I started out interviewing those four television repairmen. The interviews with snake handlers, homemakers, hobbyists, old timers and children that were once the bread and butter of local television had became rarer and rarer.

When I started at KRTV, the station was housed in a Quonset hut. When I left, it was in a million-dollar building. When I started, there was a staff of fifteen, when I left the staff had grown to more than twice that size. When I started in television there were only two local channels to choose from. When I left there were dozens of channels to choose from.

I had spent half of my life in television and I realized it was time to move on. I had no idea what I would do next, but out of the blue a dear friend, Joanne Hinch, who was my Mary Kay beauty consultant, told me she and her husband, Reverend Jim Hinch, were moving to Florida. She asked me if I would be interested in taking over some of her clients. This was an entirely new venture, but I decided it would be fun to work for myself, so I accepted her offer.

On June 6, 1988, I submitted my letter of resignation to Pete Friden, general manager of KRTV. This is what I wrote:

> *Dear Pete,*
> *The time has finally come for me to leave KRTV. I have very much enjoyed my work as a broadcaster these past twenty-six and a half years at KRTV but at this stage in my life there are other things I wish to do.*
>
> *I wish to spend more time with our grandson; to spend more relaxed time with Shirley, and to pursue a new field of endeavor as a Mary Kay Cosmetics Beauty Consultant.*
>
> *I will be willing to work until the end of the month and will help train my replacement.*
>
> *I will also be happy to offer my services to help implement the Centennial Bell project.*
>
> *I appreciate the many courtesies and opportunities you have given me at KRTV, Pete, and I will cherish the many friendships and the happy memories I have of KRTV.*

Once I made up my mind to make the change, writing the letter and giving it to Pete was not that difficult. You might say I even felt relieved. I was ready to move on. I also had given the station a month to help them make a smooth transition.

That same day, Pete Friden sent this memo to the staff of KRTV:

It is with regret that I have to announce that Norma Ashby has resigned.

Norma came to KRTV in 1962 and has served faithfully as our interviewer, our public service director, in sales, our maker of prime time specials and much more.

In twenty-six years no employee has been more loyal or dedicated to making KRTV the best.

Norma will be missed.

Her final day will be June 30.

The news of my resignation was front-page news in the *Great Falls Tribune* and in *U.S.A. Today* and was featured on KFBB-TV and KRTV News.

Here are some excerpts from that coverage and other letters I received:

In a front page story in the *Great Falls Tribune* on June 7, 1988 by Richard Ecke, Peter Friden said I was "probably the best-known face or name in Montana." Ecke wrote that I would continue to do some broadcasting work and was looking forward to spending more time with my grandson and husband.

Several days later, I was touched when I read this editorial in the *Great Falls Tribune*.

Norma has probably met more citizens, and interviewed more people, than anyone in the history of Montana broadcasting. She has been one of the state's most effective promoters. Whenever someone does a poll about influential people in the Treasure State, Ashby rates among the

A good-bye card created by Mike Halbleib, a KRTV engineer, for Norma's retirement in 1988.

Ashby family from left: daughter Ann, Shirley, Norma and son Tony at their cabin in 1988.

top ten or fifteen and is always near the head of the list of most influential women.

There isn't much this lady hasn't done. It's taken dedication and hard work. She may miss the spotlight but we at the other end of the tube will also miss something—her good cheer, her friendliness and, above all, her devotion to Montana.

There was another letter, several days later, by Scotty James of Columbia Falls, Montana, a retired editor of the *Tribune*. When I first came to Great Falls in 1961, Scotty was the editor of the paper. He was the first person I asked about a job. He had no openings at the time, but the day I started at KRTV, he called and offered me a position. It was too late. How different my life might have been if I had been a newspaper reporter instead of a broadcaster!

Scotty wrote:

The Pony Express driver swung off his perspiring horse and shouted that there was sad news for me in the river city of Great Falls.

"Norma has retired from her program and is going into private business," he said, as he gave me hell for being so hard to reach—over mountains and rivers.

"Norma can't retire," I responded. "She is just too young and she must know that Great Falls will not be the same without her."

"It was only a few days ago," I said, "that I thought the Tribune *must hire her because she had the obvious ability to become a top editor and even publisher of the* Tribune.*"*

Charlotte and I wish you the best of luck, Norma, and we hope you will enjoy your new profession.

I take my hat off to you for being such a wonderful citizen, for initiating the Russell auction, which has meant so much to the city, and for your many contributions to the city and to the state. I will never forget how you were the spark behind the Press Club.

You carved a niche in television, Norma, and one that will be virtually impossible to fill.

You will do well in your new field—and would do well in any field. I only regret that you did not join the Tribune *staff. If you had, I could say I know the new editor—or the publisher well.*

Good luck, my good friend.

Linda Caricaburu, *Great Falls Tribune* reporter, wrote me:

In the past several years, you have been a true inspiration to me to always remember the "human" side of the news...to always remember the people in our community and in our state are what the news is really all about.

Your approach to news and features has been a fine example for me and other journalists. I hate to see you leave the business, but I am sure you will continue to be a vital and vibrant force in Great Falls and throughout Montana.

Shannon Everts, a reporter for KRTV, did a piece on me for the KRTV *Evening News*. "Norma's success has come from her overwhelming curiosity and her love for people," she said. "She has brought a special taste of Montana into people's homes." When she asked me, how I would like to be remembered, I said, "I would like to be remembered as a person who loves Montana and who loves Montanans."

I laughed when Cliff Ewing, the retired general manager of KRTV, sent me this letter:

When Garryowen Broadcasting System acquired KRTV in 1969 and became the Montana Television Network, you grew and blossomed into a true Montana Personality. You may have tested and tried me, but you never disappointed me.

You really have had an exciting and inspiring broadcast career, and have provided Montana viewers with some inspirational and exciting programs. Your many scrapbooks will be a constant source of pride and reminder of your

"Norma's success has come from her overwhelming curiosity and her love for people," she said. "She has brought a special taste of Montana into people's homes."

many accomplishments and services you have provided.

One of my fondest memories of you is the statement you made to me one day after I became General Manager of KRTV. You were asking me for company financing for some endeavor you were involved in, and I had to refuse your request. In exasperation you said, "Cliff, you are the only boss I ever had who has said NO to me and has gotten away with it!"

Artist Arlene Hooker Fay sent in this tribute to the *Great Falls Tribune* on June 28, 1988:

I enjoyed the Tribune article and editorial regarding Norma Ashby's retirement from KRTV this month. But I would like to elaborate.

It has always been my understanding that Norma attended an antique auction over twenty years ago and later suggested to the Great Falls Advertising Federation that an auction would be an exciting fund-raiser, but featuring art instead.

From that idea, she and the entire ad club have continued to work to make the Russell auction a nationally known western phenomenon. She is truly an amazing example of the difference one person can make.

Charles Kuralt of CBS News wrote, "I read somewhere that you're retiring. Say it ain't so!"

Chris Stevens of Ireland, a former Great Falls newsman and author, wrote me:

No matter how blown up the male ego was, no matter how rough the political pressure, or no matter how catty the socialite might have been, you were always gracious under fire—what I would call a genuine Montana girl, and I can think of no finer compliment.

From Dorothy Floerchinger of Conrad:

The program Today in Montana *did more to build respect for our state than anything I can think of. Too many across the nation believe we are still a culturally deprived area living in the era of cowboys and Indians. But this program told of the things our people do and encouraged others to be involved, until today we have per capita more writers, visual and performing artists and people working for the common good than any other state.*

I received hundreds of cards, letters and flowers—including a dozen red roses from my husband, Shirley. It was a very heady time, with kind words coming in from all directions, accolades for a career that was built day by day, interview by interview. I was deeply humbled and grateful for this outpouring of love. At times it was emotional for me to leave behind a career I had enjoyed so much, but I also realized nothing lasts forever and the heyday of live television in which I started had been over for a long time.

Several days later, the station hosted a farewell dinner party for me at the Jack Club, a supper club in Great Falls. The entire staff was there and they presented me with a silver tray engraved with these words: "Thanks Norma for twenty-six years at KRTV." I was happy there were no long speeches.

My final day at KRTV was not as emotional as I had expected. Those who know me best have said of me that I cry when I take out the garbage. But this was not the case on my last day at the station. I had made up my mind to move on. I was happy with my past television accomplishments and I was looking forward to creating a new life for myself. I was sure I would return to KRTV from time to time for special projects.

I had typed my final remarks on the teleprompter so I could look right into the camera and wouldn't need to lower my head to read

Norma and her three grandsons: Dusty Ashby, and Jack and Bill Schrader in 1996.

them. I remembered an early piece of advice: to connect with my audience. I imagined that I was speaking directly to a family member or good friend.

As the camera light went on for the final time, I imagined I was speaking to my late mother. I said:

> Today marks my final day at KRTV as a regular employee. I would like to leave the door open to return from time to time as a guest to talk about a special project, to voice a commercial or to work on a special program or event for the station.
>
> When I started here at Channel 3 twenty-six and a half years ago, on February 19, 1962, it was the first time I had been on the air. I had had no previous TV experience. I was as green as they come to this medium. But I had two qualities that have served me well in this work. Number one, I love people. Number two, I have lots of curiosity about what makes people tick.
>
> As co-creator and co-host of the daily *Today in Montana* show with Dan Snyder, I was given the wonderful opportunity to try anything. If it worked, fine. If it didn't work, we would change it.
>
> The first ten years, we were on every morning from 8 to 9 a.m., following *The Today Show*...thus our name, *Today in Montana*. The majority of the shows were live and anything could happen.
>
> We even had a fire on the set one day. Dan said, "Keep talking. I'll grab the fire extinguisher and put it out." So as Dan frantically rushed around putting out the fire, I described his actions.
>
> We had a family of wonderful people on the show...Lou Bryant, musician; Tony Pinski, vocalist; Glenn Lockwood, newsman; and Joan Mora, exercise girl. We were all so close that we kept in touch with each other long after the show was changed.
>
> In 1972, four years after Dan Snyder had sold KRTV to Joe Sample, *Today in Montana* moved to 9 a.m. and went statewide on the Montana Television Network. We were in that position for twelve and a half years and were able to travel extensively throughout the state and had many memorable moments meeting Montanans from border to border.

But I had two qualities that have served me well in this work. Number one, I love people. Number two, I have lots of curiosity about what makes people tick.

You watched my little nephew Steve Roth grow from a performing ten-year-old on our show to a full-fledged doctor. And finally, you saw my precious grandson, Bill Schrader, make his appearance on our family Christmas show.

In the last four years, changes have come to KRTV and to my on-air work. In 1984, *Today in Montana* was moved from morning to noon. A year later, the format was changed from a magazine to a news format. Then, in 1986, the name was changed to the *Noon News*.

I am grateful to have had the many years I did have bringing you interesting people, events and projects, most of them through live television in your homes everyday.

I am constantly asked what or who was my most memorable guest. In the more than 26,000 people I have interviewed in over 7,000 shows, I guess my guests with snakes have to be the most memorable. And of all the celebrities we have interviewed, my favorite was Bob Hope.

I want to thank you all for your wonderful support over the years and for all of your cards, letters, gifts, phone calls, and personal visits wherever we have met each other.

I also want to thank the crews I have been privileged to work with these twenty-six and a half years. They are a group of fine professionals as well as great friends. We have all shared lots of laughs together and lots of tears, too.

I want to thank you for your good wishes as I embark on something entirely new. I am going to become a beauty consultant with Mary Kay Cosmetics, do some freelance journalism and perhaps you will see me back on the air from time to time promoting a special project or two.

And now thanks for watching...And have a happy day everyone. For KRTV, this is Norma Ashby reporting.

To be in the position of hostess and producer of *Today in Montana* for all of those years was a great gift and a great challenge. I will be forever grateful for the professionals I was privileged to work with, the wonderful people I interviewed, the multitude of friends I made throughout Montana, and the management who gave a woman with no on-air experience the opportunity to communicate in this special way.

To be in the position of hostess and producer of Today in Montana for all of those years was a great gift and a great challenge.

Index

Acers, Ebby Halliday 128
Aiken, George 45
Allen, Rex 43
Anderson, Evelyn 83
Anderson, Forrest H. 79, 123
Anderson-Elerding 122
Arnold, Eddy 43
Ash, Mary Kay 69-73
Ashby, Ann: See Longfellow, Ann Ashby.
Ashby, Dusty 41, 155
Ashby, Shirley 34, 38-39, 127, 137, 150, 152, 155
Ashby, Tony 40, 41
Augusta, MT 104-106
Babcock, Betty 44, 57, 83
Babcock, Tim 79, 122, 144
Baillie, Bill 77
Bartschi, Theo 105, 106
Baucus, Jean 84
Baucus, Max 113
Baumler, Ellen 84
Beery, Noah Jr. "Pidg" 43, 138
Belt, MT 104-106
Benedict, Ben 12
Bennett, Lisette 19
Bergmann, Leona 19
Berry, Jim 61
Big Sky resort 63
Blackfeet Tribe 116
Bliss, Brent 146
Bliss, Elmer 146
Blodgett, Jim 28
Bobbitt, Billie 128
Bottomly, Joe 97
Boylan, Barbara 51
Bradley, Don 19, 22, 37-38
Brennan, Walter 74
Brinkley, David 60, 64
Broadwater Hotel 107
Brock, Bruce 137
Brokaw, Tom 44
Brothers, Joyce 14
Brown, Mrs. Rdee 20-21
Bryant, Lou 17, 23, 26, 29, 30, 31, 35, 78, 156
Burgess, Bobby 34, 51
Burke, Martha 78
Bush, George H.W. 82
Bush, George W. 82
Bynum School 87
Cabot, Susan 15, 16
Cane, Bill 26
Caricaburu, Linda 153
Carpenter, Elizabeth "Liz" 50-57
Carrico, Charles 120
Carrico, Donna 120
Carter, Dan 12
Cascade County Bicentennial Committee 145-146
Cascade County Mental Health Association 142
Cascade Senior Citizens Center 130
Cascade, MT 104-106
Cash, Johnny 43, 53

Castle, Joanne 51
Chansoniers 30
Choteau, MT 104-106
Clymer, John 138
C.M. Russell Auction 43, 132-142
C.M. Russell Museum 97, 133, 137
Coburn, Walt 86
Coghlan, Ed 22-24
Cohan, Charles C. 144
Colarchek, Cyril 101-102
Compton, Lynn 19
Conners, Sheila 97-100
Conrad, MT 104-106
Cooper, Gary 75
Cornelius, Bill 129, 130
Cornelius, Shirley 129, 130, 131
Crain, Paul 9, 11, 37, 38
Craney, Ed 10
Crawford, Joan 54
Creative Casting 146
Creecy, Audrey 17, 65
Cronkite, Walter 44
Crosby, Bing 91
Crymes, Ingrid 25
Curran, Charles 123
Cushman, Dan 19
Dachs, Sam 19
Davison, Wayne 118
Day, Dennis 104
Day Child, Twila 117
De Rouche, John 116
Dean, Jimmy 43, 104
De Bries, Herb 91
DeGaulle, Charles 64
DeHavilland, Olivia 61
Del Guerra, Claire 82
DeMier, Andy 14
Deming, Bob 19
Dickerson, Nancy 17, 44
Dickinson, Angie 44
Dobie, J. Frank 133
Dodds, Ray 15
Doig, Carol 81
Doig, Ivan 81
Donaldson, Sam 44
Downs, Hugh 44
Duensing, David 110-111
Duensing, Dusty 110-111
Duensing, Nancy 110-111
Eads, George 109
Eastwood, Clint 43, 64
Ecke, Richard 151
Egan, Jay 146
Electric City Conservatory 20, 25
Elerding, Marge 19, 122
Elge, Frances 114
Elizabeth II 106-107
Ellerbee, Linda 18
Evans, Dale 43
Evening Post Pub. Co. 36, 37
Everts, Shannon 153
Ewing, Cliff 29, 37, 153-154
Fay, Arlene Hooker 154
Feiden's Flowers 20
Fields, Chester 111
First Ladies of Montana (film) 77
Fish, Andrea 40

Fleming, Lynn 103
Fleschenhar, Connie 131-132
Fliger, Roger 17-19
Floerchinger, Dorothy 105-106, 154-155
Fonda, Peter 43
Ford, Tennessee Ernie 43, 44
Forsman, Etheljean 17
Fort Benton, MT 31, 97, 104-106, 137
Fox, Pat 94
Francis, Arlene 73-76
Fraser, Willard 28
Frederick, Pauline 44
Friden, Pete 37, 38, 150-151
Furdell, Betty 17
Garryowen Broadcasting 153
Gercken, Richard 19
Gilbert, Ken 129, 131
Gilbert, Marion 129
Gilcrease Museum 114-115
Gilluly, Sam 133, 134
Ginter, Rita 25, 35
Gish, Lillian 43
Gobel, George 44, 104
Goulet, Robert 48
Great Falls Advertising Federation 48, 97, 135-142
Great Falls Gas Company 24
Great Falls Junior League 19, 43
Great Falls Press Club 104
Great Falls Tribune 151-152
Great Falls YWCA 97
Guthrie, A.B. "Bud" 34
Guy Tabacco & Sons 146
Hagener, Louis 141
Hagener, Toni 141
Halbleib, Mike; artwork by 151
Halko, Joe 111
Hamilton, George 109
Hammer, Victor 138
Hanson, Roger 146
Harper, Jack 26
Harrison, Benjamin 146
Hartman, David 34
Harvey, Paul 44, 129-132
Harwood, Tom 30
Hayden, Jeannie 11, 13, 20
Hayes, Jerome 12, 112
Helena Kiwanis Club 143
Hempl's Bakery 25, 30
Henderson, Carole 59
Hested's 14
Hibbard, Henry 28
Hibbard, Jane 28
Hildenstab, John 24, 70, 103, 105
Hinch, Jim 150
Hinch, Joanne 71, 150
Hirsh, Boyd 108
Hoefly, Ann 127-128
Hoff-Wilson, Joan 113
Holm, Celeste 43
Holmes, J.D. 37
Hope, Bob 43, 52, 75, 157
Howard, Joseph E. 144
Hoy, Chris 19
Hunt, Shirley 20
Hunter, Bob 120

Huntley, Chet 12, 59-65
Huntley, Tippy 62, 63, 64
Huntsberger, Helen 19
Hussman's Pool Hall 64
Ikeda, Tug 19, 34
Jacobson, Zella 19
James, Scotty 152-153
Johnson, Dorothy 84
Johnson, J.C. 19
Johnson, Lady Bird 50, 51, 53-57
Johnson, Luci 51
Johnson, Lyndon 47, 51, 64
Johnson, Tom 135, 136, 137
Johnston, George 141
Jones, Elsie 82, 83-85
Jones, Frieda 132
Jones, Jake 12
Judge, Carol 83
Judge, Tom 28, 32, 79, 141, 142, 145
Juedeman, Mrs. Harold 12
KARR Radio 9
KAVR Radio 89
Keenan, Nancy 143
Keller, Helen 75
Kelsey, Howard 144-145
Kennedy, John F. 64, 119-121
KFBB TV 10
KIBG Radio 27
Kimmel, John 119-120
Kinney, Thom 113
Kittredge, Jim 143
Klemencic, Richard 26, 145
KMON Radio 22
Knievel, Evel 109
Knievel, Robbie 109
Knudson, Toni 21
Kochman, Carl 19, 103, 106, 108
KOJM Radio 89
Kolman, Ed 9
KOOK TV 27-28
KPAX TV 27, 36
KQRK-FM 27
KRTV 9-42, 71, 103, 149-157
KTVQ TV 27, 36
Kuhr, Marion Broadwater 107
Kuralt, Charles 44, 63, 87, 154
KXLF TV 10, 27, 36
Laird, Melvin 127
Landers, Ann 57
Lansbury, Angela 75
Larson, Maxine Nutter 83
Last Chance Gulch (film) 77
Lawson, Joe 19, 103, 111, 116-117
Leach, Bill 103
Leeds, Lyle 90
Legowik, Matt 12
Lennon Sisters 51
Lentfer, Hank 100
Lilly, George 36, 37
Lincoln, Don 111
Lind, Bob 34-35, 98
Linkletter, Art 16-17
Lockwood, Cory 26
Lockwood, Edna 11, 13, 20
Lockwood, Glenn 17, 21, 23, 26, 29, 35, 156

Longfellow, Ann Ashby 40, 41
Love, Elizabeth 19
Lovelace, Ed 89
Lucken, Mary Ellen 19
Luinstra, Tim 19, 103, 111
Lynde, Stan 28, 31, 143
McCartney, Clay 92, 95
McCartney, Maida 89-96
McCoo, Marilyn 43
McDaniel, Larry 20
McDaniel, Marilyn 20
McIntire, John 44
McKay, Malcolm S. "Bud" 138
McLaughlin, John 28
McNay, Lindsay 103
Magner, Betty 31
Mann, Walt 20
Mansfield, Mike 31, 61, 94
Margaret, Princess 42, 123-125
Marianetti, Gene 22
Marlenee, Ron 113
Marquand, Ian 103
Marsh, Veta 105, 106
Martin, Dick 146
Martz, Judy 82-83
Mathison, Carol 123
Mathison, Grenfell 123
Matthews, Lee 30
Mehmke, Ella 31-32, 41, 54, 129
Mehmke, Walter 39
Meier, June 19
Melcher, John 113
Melton, Terry 134
Merrill, Robert 43
Metcalf, Donna 28, 32
Metcalf, Lee 28, 32
Meyer, Jane 146
Micone, Mike 28
Miles City Bucking Horse Sale 108
Milk River Wagon Train 28
Millard, Larry 20
Miller, Rita: See Ginter, Rita.
Milsap, Ronnie 43
Mimnaugh, Terry 112-113, 114
Moe, Barbara 122
Monkman, Olga 105-106
Montana Bicentennial Commission 145-148
Montana Capitol Centennial 148
Montana Centennial Band 77-78
Montana Centennial Train 144-145
Montana Cowbelles 104
Montana Deaconess Medical Center 57
Montana Federation of Garden Clubs 140
Montana Historical Society 84, 143, 146
Montana School for the Deaf and the Blind 19
Montana State Fair 43, 103-104
Montana state fish 140-142
Montana Statehood Centennial 82, 146-148
Montana Television Network 22, 23, 26, 27, 28, 36, 83, 147-148, 153, 156
Montana Territorial Centennial 38-39, 42, 57, 144-146
Montana, Montie, Jr. 62

Montgomery, George 43-44, 138
Montgomery, Joe 36
Moore, Stu 105-106
Mora, Jerri 26
Mora, Joan 17, 23, 26, 29, 156
Mora, Joanne 26
Morgan, Bob 33, 34, 138
Morgan, Mary 125
Morris, Joe 105-106
Mort, Denise 36
Mortag, Kenny 134
Morton, Rogers 70
Murphy, Audie 15, 16
Murray, Ann 43
Myers, Fred 114-115
Myers, Rex C. 143
Nabors, Jim 43
Neal, Patricia 57
Nehru, Jawaharlal 64
Nelson, Van Kirke 136-137
Nett, Art 105-106
Nixon, Pat 28, 42, 43, 70, 127
Nixon, Richard 127
North American Indian Days 115-117
Nugent, Pat 51
O'Connor, Carroll 44
Old Person, Doris 117
Old Person, Earl 93, 97, 116, 117
Old Person, George 116
Olson, Carey 103
Olson-Stratford, Audrey: See Creecy, Audrey.
O'Neill, Thomas "Tip" 113, 114
Orduno, Robert 146
Osgood, Charles 44
Osmond Brothers 43
Osmond, Marie 43
Otis, Maxine 24
Oz the Clown 100-101
PageWerner Architects 29
Paladin, Vivian 84
Paris, The (store) 25
Parrot, The (store) 110-111
Pasma, Jim 111
Pauley, Jane 44, 45
Peale, Mrs. Norman Vincent 67
Peale, Norman Vincent 43, 67
Pearson, John 19
Perkins, Ira 87
Perspective on Great Falls 14, 36
Peters, Roberta 43
Philip, Prince 106
Phillips, Jeanne 59
Phillips, Pauline Friedman: See Van Buren, Abigail.
Pickens, Slim 138
Pinski, Loren 26
Pinski, Tony 17, 23, 26, 29, 30, 31, 35, 156
Pomeroy, Lyndon 29
Poor, Jim 19
Post, Mrs. W.R. "Postie" 110
Preston, Bill 38
Price, Vincent 47
Pride, Charley 28, 34, 46, 138
Pride, Rozene 46, 138
Pullar, Shari 20
Pyle, Denver 44, 138

Racicot, Marc 82
Racicot, Theresa 83
Ralston, J.K. "Ken" 85-89
Rankin, Jeannette 112-114
Raty, Jack 134, 137
Reagan, Ronald 52, 75, 121-122
Remington, Frederic 115
Renner, Fred 133, 134, 136, 138, 140
Renner, Ginger 138
Retton, Mary Lou 44
Reynolds, Bennie 104
Richardson, Elliott 127, 128
Riddle, Dick 94
Ritter, Russell J. 37
Robertson, Dale 44
Rockwell, Bob 138
Rogers, Roy 43, 72
Roosevelt, Eleanor 76
Ross, Pete 61
Roth, Amalia 40
Roth, Annemarie 38, 39
Roth, Bill 111
Roth, Joel 40
Roth, Julianna 40
Roth, Steve 26, 39-40, 157
Rothenbuehler, Susie 20, 102
Ruby, Bob 94
Russell, Charles M. 86, 114, 115, 123-124, 127, 135, 139-140; on himself 134-135; statue of 112-113
Russell, Jack 138, 139-142
Russell, Lucille 138, 139, 140
Russell, Nancy 139, 140
Sagunsky, Caroline 72
Salinger, Pierre 121
Salmon Lake 111
Sample, Joe 22, 26, 27-28, 29, 33, 36, 37, 156
Samson, Bill 135, 136, 137
Sanger, Jim 91
Schmidt, Grover 105, 106
Schmidt, Margaret 144
Schrader, Bill 41, 155, 157
Schrader, Jack 41, 117, 155
Schultz, Wayne 20, 105
Schwinden, Jean 81
Schwinden, Ted 34, 79, 80-81, 83, 113-114
Scott, Willard 34
Scriver, Bob 97, 138
Seltzer, O.C. 115
Seltzer, Steve 138
Shelby, MT 104-106
Sherman, Bill 138, 143
Sievers, Joanna Lester 30
Skelton, Red 44
Smith, Ed 28
Smith, Juliet 125
Smith, Margaret Chase 44-50
Smithsonian Institution 110
Snyder, Dan 9-10, 11, 12, 13, 15, 16, 23, 26-27, 30, 35, 37, 104, 105, 156
Solberg, Eileen 19
Sons & Daughters of Montana Pioneers 147-148
Sparrow, Barney 133
Sparrow, Claris 133

Stahl, LeRoy 19, 134
Stahl, Leslie 44
Stanish, John 24-25
Stanton, Frank 123
Stark, Joe 103
Starodomskaya, Svetlana 18, 19
Steinbeck, John 144-145
Stephens, Ann 82, 83
Stephens, Stan 82, 147
Stephenson, Nancy 19
Stevens, Chris 19, 77, 154
Stevenson, Branson 136
Stone, Irving 65
Sullivan, Annie 75
Symbols of Montana (booklet) 143-144
Taillon, Cy 108
Taiple, Denys 78
Taylor, Barbara 11, 13, 17
Thayer, Gene 146
Thomas, Marlo 44
Thoreson, Nels 141
Three Young Men 94
Tilton, Dan 26
Tilton, George 18, 26, 29
Tilton, Laurie 26
Tilton, Scott 26
Tintinger, Alice 32, 35
Today in Montana (show), history of 12-42
Townsend, Juliet 125
Trapp, Maria von 65-68
Trebesch, Helen 19
Turner, Jim 103
Urton, Marliss 20
USA Today 151-152
Valier, MT 105-106
Van Buren, Abigail 57-59
Viking Shop 25, 35
Vorhauer, Bruce 111-112
Wally's Superette 24-25
Walters, Barbara 44, 75
Warden, Margaret 141, 142
Weaver, John 112-113
Weismann, Evelyn 25, 32, 35
Welch, Abbie 133
White House 50-52
White, Lucille 19
Whitney, Art 142
Whitsitt, Bill 22
Wilcox, Marty 19
Willett, Robert V., Jr. 145
Williams, Pat 113
Wilson, Dave 146
Wirth, Craig 18, 19
Wolf, Nita 19
Wolverton, Jack 61
Woodahl, Bob 133
Woody, Bob 129
Wraalstad, Karen 65
Yellowstone Boys Ranch 28
Young, Babe 19
Young Running Crane, Sam 116
Ypma, Janice 101
Zimmerman, Dan 88
Zion, Scotty 147
Zonta 127

Norma Beatty Ashby is a fourth-generation Montanan. Born in Helena, she was raised on a ranch near Winston, Montana and attended a one-room schoolhouse on Beaver Creek. After graduating from Helena High School in 1953, she received a bachelor's degree in journalism from the University of Montana in 1957. After three summers of working at Helena's *Independent Record*, she went to New York where she worked as a picture researcher for *LIFE* Magazine and *MD Medical Newsmagazine*.

In 1961, Norma returned to Montana, and in early 1962 she got a job as hostess and producer of KRTV's *Today in Montana* show. It was a job she loved for the next twenty-four years. During that time, she wrote twenty-one television documentaries, including *Last Chance Gulch*, which is narrated by Chet Huntley, and *First Ladies of Montana*. She co-authored, with Rex Myers, *Symbols of Montana*. She also wrote two essays entitled "What Is A Montanan?" and "The Montana Women," both of which were printed in the Congressional Record. In 1986, she became an interviewer for KRTV's *Noon News* as well as public service director, and special projects director for the station.

During her time at KRTV, she received a number of awards. The Greater Montana Foundation named *Today in Montana* TV Program of the Year in 1963, 1964, 1965 and 1967. In the 1980s, the Montana Broadcasters Association gave Norma six awards, including TV Program of the Year for the twentieth anniversary show of *Today in Montana* in 1982 and the TV Broadcaster of the Year Award in 1985. In 1984, she was selected by a poll taken by the *Great Falls Tribune*, as the most influential woman in Great Falls. In 2004, she was selected for the Great Falls YWCA's 2004 Salute to Women in the category of creative arts and communication.

Since 1988, she has worked as a freelance journalist and broadcaster and as a beauty consultant for Mary Kay Cosmetics.

She has been married to Shirley Carter Ashby, a retired banker and third-generation Montanan since 1964. They have a son, a daughter and three grandsons. Norma enjoys their cabin at Lincoln, as well as fishing, reading, writing, and studying Montana history.